ON

A SOCIAL H
THE LONDON BUS

Edited by David Lawrence

With contributions by
Laurie Akehurst, Leon Daniels, Roger French,
Oliver Green, David Lawrence, Sam Mullins,
Simon Murphy, Richard Peskett, Tim Shields,
Mike Sutcliffe, Roger Torode, Caroline Warhurst

Published in 2014

London Transport Museum
Covent Garden Piazza
London WC2E 7BB
Tel +44 (0)20 7379 6344

Designed by LTM Design

Printed by
Pureprint Group, Uckfield UK
pureprint.com

ISBN 978-1-871829-23-5
ltmuseum.co.uk
Registered charity number 1123122

Picture credits
Sources for images are as indicated in
individual captions. Where a number is
given as the reference, the images are © TfL,
from the London Transport Museum collection.

CONTENTS

FOREWORD

As part of Transport for London's Year of the Bus celebrations in 2014, we invited a group of experts with a passion for the London bus to share their thoughts on its evolution and impact on the capital. This book is the result of that collaboration and we are delighted to have worked with our contributors to produce a unique assessment of a much loved icon.

Since the mid-19th century, the humble omnibus has been the unsung hero of transport in London. Originally a horse-drawn box on wheels with no upper deck or ventilation, it has now become the sleek, highly-efficient form of mass transit that we know and love. Buses have continuously adapted: the internal combustion engine has replaced the horse, and in these environmentally aware times, the latest diesel-electric hybrid vehicles can emit cleaner air than they take in. Now we benefit not only from a roof over our heads but also get thoroughly spoilt by heating and cooling. This evolution was never revolution, but its progress always reflected changes in society and industry as much as vehicle technology.

In the mid-20th century, before the private car became a serious challenge to the established life of the city, buses took workers to work, children to school, and shoppers to the high street. During the week, London's factories and industry were supplied by a workforce delivered by bus. As Londoners sought weekend relief from the smoggy grind, the bus opened up trips to the countryside, and took crowds to and from sporting events. When Londoners moved into the suburbs and car ownership increased, the resulting decline in bus passengers drove demands for increased efficiencies and the bus conductor became an endangered species.

Fortunately the decline was arrested. Political change, limited roadspace and environmental concerns drove a renaissance of the London bus. The city did not invest in more carriageway or more parking. Instead bus priority lanes, cheaper fares and significant investment succeeded in growing patronage. From an all-time low in the 1990s, ridership grew strongly in the first decade of the 21st century. By the early years of the second decade it had returned to the sort of volumes we enjoyed in the late 1950s and, it seems, is destined to continue tracking London's inexorable population growth.

One thing hasn't changed for the past 185 years: as each day dawns, the buses venture out to carry Londoners about their business. As always, success is judged by the day being uneventful. As sure as water comes out of the tap, or electricity comes down the line, iconic London's buses come down the road and take you where you need to go.

We hope you will enjoy this book, which brings together acknowledged authorities for particular periods in the development of the London bus. Transport for London and the London Transport Museum are very grateful for the welcome participation of these writers, who have each contributed a personal and historical perspective to the continuing narrative, of how the bus has kept London moving.

Leon Daniels
Managing Director, Surface Transport, Transport for London

The first 'bus' that trainee drivers encountered at the former London Transport Chiswick training school was this painted wood mock-up. One of the specialist driving instructors directs a new recruit.
2003/7437

Introduction

David Lawrence and Sam Mullins

2014 is Year of the Bus, a landmark year for several reasons. The London General Omnibus Company (LGOC), which became part of London Transport and forms a substantial part of Transport for London's heritage, operated its first mechanical buses in London in 1904. A decade later it sent almost 1,300 buses to serve overseas in the First World War. The last horse buses ran in London between 1914 and 1916. In 1924, the London Traffic Act began the process of regulating London bus operation which would lead to the London Transport monopoly within a decade.

CELEBRATING THE BUS

The very first version of London's world-leading Routemaster bus was unveiled in 1954, the same year that the last examples of the earlier classic bus type - the 'RT' - were ordered. London Transport, direct predecessor to Transport for London, opened its ground breaking bus overhaul works at Aldenham, Hertfordshire, in 1954 too. In 1994 the former London bus network was sold off to private operators. 2004 saw the replacement of many remaining Routemasters by other vehicles on London services. In 2014 one of the original B type buses has been restored to working order by the London Transport Museum, and travelled to revisit sites of the First World War, as part of the Museum's 'Goodbye Piccadilly' exhibition programme.

This book is a social history of the London bus. Featuring the expertise of curators, historians, planners and transport commissioners, it offers a comprehensive study of the bus as a vitally important social and economic presence in the metropolis. Rail-bound trams, and trolleybuses attached to fixed networks of overhead wires, were never permitted to penetrate the West End or City areas. As mass carriers for citizens of London's inner suburbs for several decades until complete replacement by buses in 1962: they are part of our story too.

We begin by taking the reader on a thematic journey to consider the phenomenon of the London bus: its design; the men and women who operated and maintained the buses; the experience of riding the bus; the presence of the bus in the streets of the city; and the bus as internationally recognised icon of London. To conclude this essay, we look to the future of the London bus, and introduce the chapters which follow it.

Celebrating the London Bus

Classic Design
Designer: Mini Moderns®
© Transport for London 2014
**Copies of this poster are available from
London Transport Museum shop, Covent Garden Piazza**
ltmuseumshop.co.uk

MAYOR OF LONDON

**TRANSPORT
FOR LONDON**
EVERY JOURNEY MATTERS

HORSE TO HYDROGEN: MAKING THE BUS

The London bus is older than the Tube. George Shillibeer (1797–1866) began his Paddington to Bank omnibus service 185 years ago in 1829. Shillibeer chose the Latin word omnibus, meaning 'for all', to proclaim his horse-drawn vehicles as the first transport mode available to anyone from any class having money for the fare. In doing so, we got the abbreviation 'bus' which is now recognised internationally. Not only were Shillibeer's omnibuses available to anyone with the fare, his passengers did not need to pre-book their travel, but simply hailed a vehicle by raising an arm to attract the driver's attention and climbed on board. Early routes were identified by a system of livery colours, with some destinations painted on the vehicles sides. As we shall see in this book, the brothers Herbert and Albert Reinohl recorded these liveries in meticulous detail.[1] From 1905, red buses began to dominate the street scene.

Undergoing continuous improvements in technology, safety and comfort, buses have changed from small, open topped horse drawn vehicles to highly designed, sophisticated pieces of technology. They have been powered by petrol, diesel oil, steam and electricity; the most recent advance being hydrogen fuel cell technology, which produces zero pollution.

Emerging from the same carpenters' workshops as private carriages and agricultural vehicles, early buses were fashioned from wood and painted by hand. The first mechanical buses continued to have craftsman-made bodies, placed onto factory produced chassis with motors. London's buses were for many years designed and made especially for London. The London General Omnibus Company created a successful commercial business - the Associated Equipment Company (AEC) - to manufacture buses and other vehicles for London and to supply an international market. This in-house capability meant buses were increasingly standardised in both manufacture and maintenance - perfect for a massive and intensive network where reliability was essential. Contractors, including Weymann Motor Bodies Ltd,[2] and Park Royal Vehicles,[3] produced vehicle superstructures to London Transport designs. Engineer A A M Durrant (1889–1984)[4] worked with designer Douglas Scott (1913–1990) to produce technically and aesthetically brilliant vehicles for the everyday work of moving millions around the city and its countryside. Styling of streamlined buses and trolleybuses of the 1930s and 1950s took advantage of developments in metal shaping from the motorcar and aircraft industries. Relaxation of controls on the size of buses which could be operated in London streets, and rapid design innovation produced successive standard types.

The London bus has waged war at home and overseas. Twice, vehicles from elsewhere came to the aid of London, bringing the geography of unusual names and colours to our thoroughfares. These examples form part of the story too. Using bus chassis, other vehicles were made for special roles, such as staff canteens and roadside repair units. A bus overhaul works was established at Chiswick, West London, in the 1920s to create an economical, centralised maintenance facility. This was supplemented by the massive Aldenham Bus Overhaul Works in Hertfordshire, from 1956. After the Routemaster, no further buses were designed especially for London until the New Bus for London, or New Routemaster.

To give an illustration of bus design and development, many of the standard types produced or operated by the London General Omnibus Company, London Transport, and Transport for London, are shown on this page spread and the one that follows. Vehicle evolution was both technical and aesthetic, governed by regulations for vehicle size and carrying capacity, and contemporary attitudes to the safety of passengers, crews, pedestrians and other road users. Buses were adapted for special functions such as long-distance operation or restricted bridge heights: these are represented by the variations of RT, RF and RM types.

B 1910

K 1919

NS 1923

S 1920

ST 1930

STL 1932

 Q 1932

LT 1929

T 1929

RT 1939

TF 1939

RTW 1948

RTL 1948

TD 1946

XA 1966

RLH 1950

RM LATE PRODUCTION

RM EARLY PRODUCTION

STD 1946

DMS 1970

MBS 1964

HYDROGEN FUEL CELL BUS 2010

RMC 1962

RF COACH 1966

TITAN 1977

RM1 PROTOTYPE 1954

RF BUS 1952

RM2 1954

NEW ROUTEMASTER 2012

London Transport's first trained craftswoman, Christine Oliver, employed at the Aldenham Bus Overhaul Works in 1981, stripping vehicle floors and making seat cushions. Christine rests her hands on an array of moquette seat fabrics, accompanied by her tools. In the background is what appears to be a sofa upholstered in transport textiles.
2006/7161

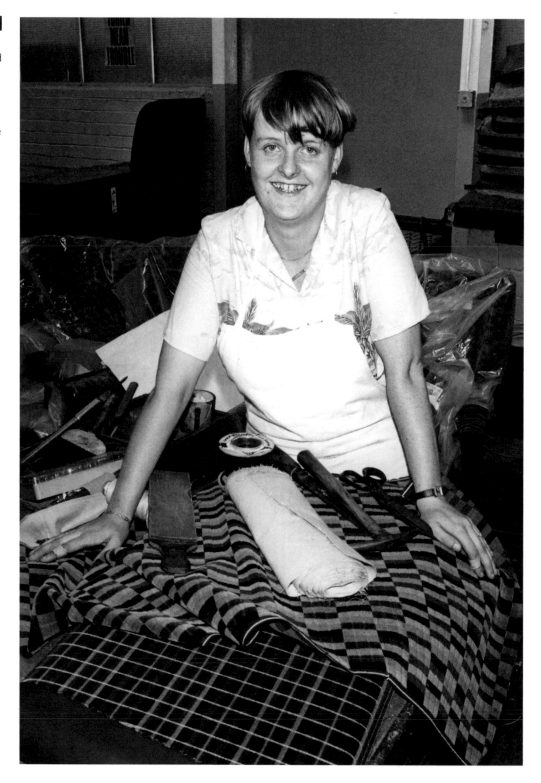

A Routemaster bus being overhauled at Aldenham Works in the 1970s. At Aldenham, bus bodies were separated from their chassis for transfer to separate areas for repair, replacement and overhaul.
2002/18956

CREWING THE BUS

London bus crews have an historical reputation for humour and wit, underpinned by fortitude and a sense of service. The face of the conductor standing on the rear platform was for millions of tourists the face of London. 'One Man Operation' - the driver taking the fares - came to London from 1968. Conductors either transferred or retired, whilst some retrained to become drivers. Now the driver, and on the New Routemaster the conductor too, represent the organisation. Buses have been crewed by ex-tram and trolleybus drivers, young people starting on life-long careers towards management, and transient workers wanting a real flavour of the city. Women joined the front line of the road transport systems during two world wars, and direct recruits from the Caribbean, Ireland and elsewhere, came to work on the bus networks from the early 1950s. Now, new Londoners staffing the buses come from many global locations and cultures.

London Transport crews were identified by their military-style uniforms and coloured cap badges - blue/white for central Buses, red for Trams and Trolleybuses, green for Country Buses & Coaches. At the roadside, bus inspectors - promoted from vehicle operating staff - helped to keep the service regulated. A centralised training school employed instructors and examiners to train and test new recruits, or prepare them for new vehicles, different tasks, and promotion. Each of these senior roles was identified by a special cap badge, again colour-coded. Teams of skilled mechanics worked at the bus garages with cleaners and bill posters to keep the buses in good order; there were even dedicated fire prevention teams. Staff benefited from philanthropic welfare schemes, subsidised canteens selling food cooked by London Transport chefs, and staff associations covering everything from flying light aircraft to fishing, amateur dramatics to athletics. There were beauty competitions for female conductresses and Christmas parties for children of transport staff.

The London bus driver as enthusiastic guide to the city is represented in this cartoon figure drawn by Ray Tooby during the 1950s for use on publicity material.

David Lawrence collection

To promote the 1951 Festival of Britain, four RT type buses made a goodwill tour of Europe. Starting in Norway, the itinerary included Sweden, Denmark and Holland before ending in France. Tour staff greet the crowds in Brussels, Belgium. There were seven staff, led by Frank Forsdick, a foreman at Aldenham. The drivers, who were also engineering staff in case of breakdown, were Fred Boxall, Arthur Buckerfield, Arthur Oakes and J Brooks. Another mechanic, Bill Stephens, and an electrician, George Sharp, also went along. In an interview with the *London Transport Magazine*, Stephens recalled, 'It was a dream come true, we were treated like kings.'

1998/52121

Pauline Bartley a 23 year old conductor from Stockwell Garage (who served on bus route 88 between Mitcham and Acton Green) is crowned 'London Transport's Gala Charm Girl' of 1977 by LT Chairman, the Right Honourable Kenneth Robinson PC. Miss Bartley was selected from sixty contestants by a panel of judges that included the Mayor and Mayoress of Hounslow, Fulham FC manager Bobby Campbell and BBC Radio London personality Susie Barnes at an open air event at Osterley Sports Ground.

1998/87213

Photographer Julia Spiegl created a portfolio of bus staff portraits for London Transport Museum in 1989. In this view, conductor Jennifer Griffith (badge number N28044) wears her summer uniform, and Gibson ticket-issuing machine, on the boarding platform of a Routemaster bus. Jennifer Griffith was a conductor on route 73.

2005/9753

The many roles performed by London buses' public-facing staff were identified by bar and circle cap badges for many decades. Derived from the London General Omnibus Company brass 'winged wheel' badge, London Transport colour-coded badges to denote the fleet in which the individual worked, and the specific duty to which they were allocated. The more senior staff wore larger, decorated badges, with coloured central segments or a wreath of laurel leaves. The creatures supporting each end of the bar and circle on the more elaborate badges are griffins - mythical beasts which formed part of the London Transport corporate identity for some decades. Badges from top left to bottom right: Tram and Trolleybus conductor instructor (mid-1950s–1962); Green Line controller (c1960s–1970); Green Line chief inspector (c1959–70); London General Omnibus Company driver and conductor (c1910–1920); prototype bus crew badge (1967); Tram and Trolleybus senior inspector (1933–50), later used as Central Bus senior inspector (c1950–1978); Tram and Trolleybus driving instructor (1942–1962); Central Bus chief examiner (c1942–1966); bus fleet fireman (late 1930s–1950s); Central Buses Divisional Mechanical Inspector (1933–85); Central Buses Assistant Chief Instructor (c1942–c1985); Country Buses & Coaches driver and conductor (1933–70).

Images David Lawrence collection

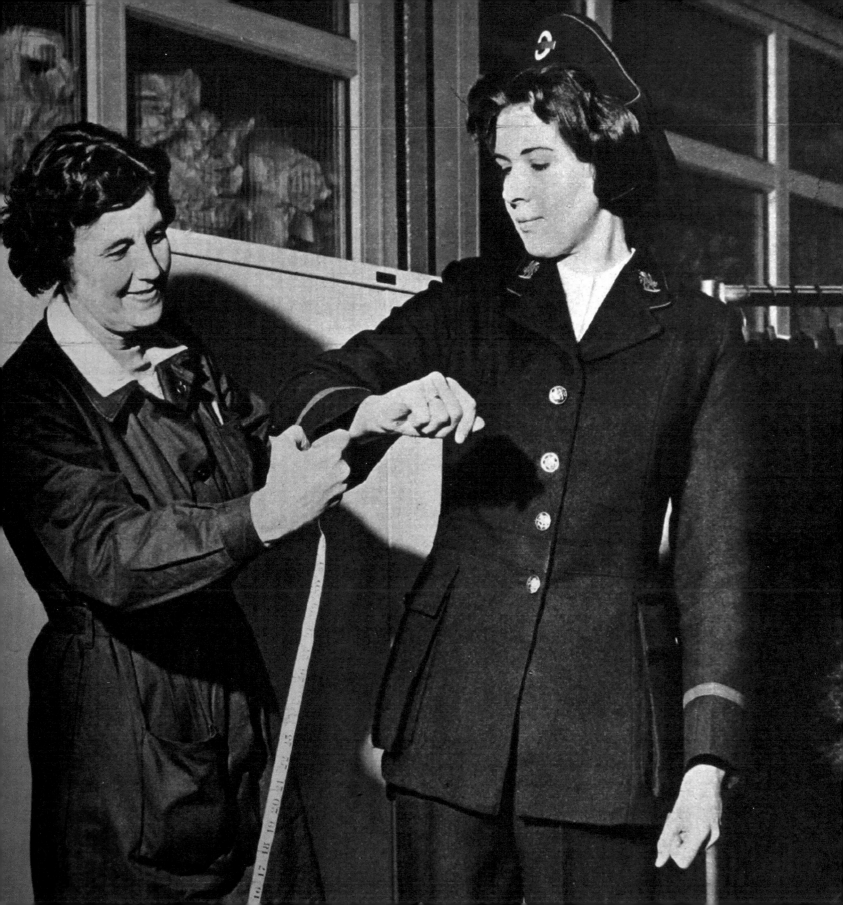

RIDING THE BUS

Part of our social history as Londoners and visitors is the sensory experience of riding on a bus, through the intimate centre of the capital (never penetrated by trams or trolleybuses), and out into its country roads. We will have different ideas of this depending on our age, but one overall impression stands in for all London's classic buses - they have a distinctive effect on the senses. For much of the twentieth century, the passenger's experience was based on double deck, open rear platform vehicles. The pleasure and convenience of hopping on and off a bus in teeming streets was a thrill of London life. (It was a trick of young Londoners to see if the conductor was busy taking fares on the upper deck, and ride just far enough on the open platform to avoid buying a ticket.)

Then there was the first touch of the fingers on the grab pole wrapped in ribbed plastic as we climbed onto the rear platform, or steadied ourselves in the moving vehicle. The next choice was seat location. Early buses provided an enclosed lower deck, and an exposed upper level, with precarious outside stairs. Accessibility was very poor by present standards, reflecting somewhat different attitudes to social inclusion which would be unacceptable today. Longitudinal seats near the entrance were useful for short trips and to watch life on the bus: passengers with parcels might sit here too. From here travellers could observe the mystery of the conductor's cubby hole and position of control: its fare table, locker and time-keeping card. The rows of bench seats all gave a reasonable view out to the street, but the best one was to the left behind the driver where children could pretend to direct the bus themselves. Standing downstairs was not ideal as the conductor would need to move up and down the bus. Upstairs, the choice was between cosy mischief in the back seat, or a panoramic view of the streetscape from the front, interrupted only by the conductor coming up to take fares or adjust the destination blind.

Further sensations have permeated historical encounters with London's buses. We have seen how the conductor was the central figure overseeing and animating the bus. Many helped passengers far beyond their remit, others were beautiful singers or sharp comedians. All knew the streets they plied. For passengers, the sound of coins in the conductor's leather pouch and the tickets reeled out with the click of a ratchet from a bright aluminium machine mounted on a tinkling leather and webbing harness, are as much the essence of London travel as those 'mind the gap' announcements on the Tube.

Advertising panels commissioned from leading graphic artists to promote safe travel or London landmarks, gave colourful highlights to the dark red, cream and green interiors. The white rings of 'PUSH ONCE' bell pushes, and the Johnston lettering of notices, stood out against the red. Coloured moquette fabrics created by industrial designers were crafted to remain bright even after heavy use, and echoed the most avant garde of European modernist textiles. Now, many of our bus interiors are blue, yellow and orange - bright colours to aid visual perception. With its sumptuous red, silver and gold interiors, the New Routemaster gives us an updated sense of our heritage.

We know the joy of a seat to ourselves, and the touch of seat fabric against bare summer legs and winter coats. We note the peculiar smells on the bus: not the passengers or their luggage, but that oddly London bouquet of aromas coming from the bus itself. For the present, plastics offer a clean, synthetic background scent, but London's RT and Routemasters could be recognised by odour alone: the oily Rexine imitation leathercloth wall covering, and the dusty wool-nylon of moquette over seat foam. Hot light bulbs warmed the primrose paint of the metal interiors to emit a unique smell, while the window frames and glasses had their own melancholy scent on a cold day. Upstairs, where smokers enjoyed hazy dominance until 1991, the remnants of many time-passing cigarettes mingled with discarded paper tickets to produce a particular olfactory sensation.

Distinctive sounds introduce another dimension of experience. We will know the noise of the engine and transmission somewhere below or behind us, the grinding pull-away from the stop and the shriek of the brakes, punctuated by the bell to stop and start buses with a conductor and the slap of the bell cord on the ceiling if pulled too hard. To support greater accessibility for everyone, bells have mostly given way to electronic bleeps, accompanied by digital voices and LED displays announcing bus stops or giving instructions.

Buses make London legible and the huge territory of the metropolis navigable. At first, when literacy was not commonplace and bus competition was widespread, horse buses were painted in a range of colourful liveries to indicate their operator and route. With better co-ordination, regular bus services were given numbers. Country buses on new satellite networks helped create the post-1945 new towns such as Harlow and Stevenage, and continued to operate as part of London Transport until 1970. Green Line coaches gave Londoners rapid connections to much of the Home Counties, and to transport hubs like Heathrow Airport. From 1968, routes were substantially and progressively altered, and the scale of bus operations was reduced, as a result of the *Bus Reshaping Plan* 1966, drafted to address problems including staff shortages, traffic congestion, increased private car ownership, and the need for cost savings.[5] A significant result of this plan was the comprehensive introduction of one-man operated buses, and the new express Red Arrow city centre network.

Transport for London and its heritage constituents have always produced guides to the road vehicle system. Folder maps brought several hundred miles of routes together in pocket-sized compendiums, from which we can see that some routes have barely changed over a century, while others are quite new. The history of these bus maps is a cartographic, typographic and pictorial study in itself, revealing the changing morphology of London alongside the evolution in design aesthetics and printing techniques. There were leaflets too called *London from a bus top*. Booklet guides covered many places of interest such as street markets and churches. Quick to realise the potential of lucrative tourist audiences, London Transport trained special Tour Guides to give mobile commentaries, sometimes in a number of languages.

A selection of the printed folder maps issued free to travellers on London Transport's bus, Tram and Trolleybus and Green Line coach networks. The graphic style of these maps remained consistent from the late 1940s to 1970. 'Hop on a Bus' was a campaign to encourage bus travel at a time when passenger levels were falling. *London from a bus top* promoted this cheap, elevated position to the advantage of tourists and Londoners by detailing some of the major landmarks. Conducted Coach Tours were operated alongside scheduled bus services until the mid-1980s, visiting city locations and historic places on the fringes of London such as Windsor Castle.

During the hot summer of 1976, a bus conductor, wearing summer uniform, checks the Go-As-You-Please season tickets offered for inspection by a couple and their young daughter on the upper deck of a Routemaster bus. The seats are upholstered with the tartan-style moquette designed specifically for the Routemaster by industrial designer Douglas Scott.

2001/5627

THE BUS IN THE STREET

It is impossible now to imagine the London street scene without knowing that moment as the red bus looms in the distance, and we think 'is it my number?' and try to read the route on the back-lit destination blinds. From the early 1920s, routes were divided into stages and sections marked by special signs and posts. These stop 'flags' became small pieces of industrial art, created by architects Charles Holden (1875–1960) and Christian Barman (1898–1980), and designer Hans Schleger (1898–1976). Schleger's proposals included the potential for combining red (buses), blue (trams) and green (coaches) graphic and typographic motifs, with distinctive stop post finials based on prototypes from New York's bus systems. Every part of the bus stop post, sign and finial was made in London.

Bus stations have formed community hubs across the capital. These might provide interchange between rail and road, or the starting point for long-distance journeys. Architecture has made many bus stations distinctive locations in urban regeneration from Southgate (1932) to Canada Water (1999), Vauxhall (2005) and Stratford City (2011).

Buses are moving advertisements for themselves, and for many commercial products and activities. Historically they carried publicity for medicinal cures and theatre shows. Newspapers, holiday destinations, Ideal Home Exhibitions, sporting and gambling promotions, faith events and feature films have all taken a turn on these prominent mobile billboards. From 1969, experiments were made with covering buses in painted murals. With the inception of perforated film graphics, the entire back of a bus including the windows can be safely used to create a unique moving advertisement. Now, the red bus is seen as a familiar, reassuring presence amongst the many visual distractions that compete for attention in our cityscape.

Before London Transport settled upon a standard form of stop 'flag' sign in the mid-1930s - similar to that still in use today - the organisation experimented with a range of post and sign designs. Hans Schleger proposed the graphics, and the terrazzo concrete posts - once a rich shade of pink - were partially designed by in-house publicity officer Christian Barman. This display was staged at the London Transport Building Department works in Parson's Green, west London in 1936.
1998/52358

BUS AS ICON

Around the world, London buses have been ambassadors for the capital. They have served through three Olympic Games (1908, 1948, 2012) and two Commonwealth Games (1911, 1934),[6] More than 900 London buses carried troops around France, and as far as Germany, during the Great War of 1914-18 - mobile reminders of home and loved ones. London Transport sent its red buses to North America on a number of occasions, to promote tourism in Britain. A red double decker was central to the Closing Ceremony of the 2008 Olympic Games in Beijing, where the Mayor of London received the Olympic flag to begin the journey to the London 2012 Olympiad.

The coincidence of cheap colour printing with the rise of tourism in post-war London, and the demise of trams and trolleybuses, ensured that internal combustion buses found a place as the visual focus of millions of tourist postcards and publications. No view of Whitehall or Oxford Street could fail to be enhanced by the inclusion of at least one big red bus. Images of Piccadilly Circus and Trafalgar Square often featured several buses in glorious procession around the traffic islands - primary icons of the metropolis.

For those who have not encountered a London bus in real life, the bus features in fiction too, as a place where characters reflect on their lives and loves: in Virginia Woolf's *Mrs Dalloway* (1925), character Elizabeth Dalloway experiences the modern city at Victoria, where 'buses swooped, settled, were off – garish caravans glistening with red and yellow varnish…She took a seat on top… She was delighted to be free…it was like riding, to be rushing up Whitehall'. There have been several virtual appearances too. Cliff Richard drove an RT in the film *Summer Holiday* (1962). Another RT was central to the childrens' television series *Here Come the Double Deckers* (1970-71).[7] In J K Rowling's 'Harry Potter' films (2004-), the magical triple-deck Knight Bus is fashioned from two RT bodies. The English situation comedy *On the Buses* (1969 – 73) gave rise to three films, two of which featured red double deck buses.[8]

Retired London buses have been exported to many parts of the world to carry on their routine work of passenger movement, or to promote tourism in 'Visit Britain' campaigns. Others have been bought, or indeed brought back from overseas, by enthusiasts for restoration. This labour of love means Londoners can still enjoy rides back through time. Transport for London supports a fleet of Routemasters running on route 15 through the city.[9]

Collectable pin badges have become a standard feature of international sports events. For the London 2012 Olympic and Paralympic Games, a myriad of symbols were produced for sale. One of the more obvious themes represented was the London bus which travelled to Beijing with Mayor of London Boris Johnson, to receive the Olympic flag.
David Lawrence collection

London buses guarantee immediate recognition for any narrative, however incredible. The 1958 edition of R C Sherriff's *The Cataclysm* imagined buses caught in a flood beside St Paul's Cathedral after the Moon collided with the Earth.
David Lawrence collection

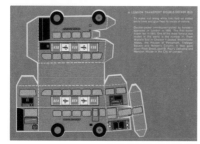

Around 1968, writer and journalist on design matters Corin Hughes-Stanton, and experimental filmmaker Stephen Dwoskin, hoped to make some money and entertain children by creating a number of postcards which could be cut-out and assembled into models. They chose various transport subjects, including this stylised Routemaster bus advertising British European Airways.
David Lawrence collection

BUSES OF THE FUTURE

With greater co-ordination of service operators ensuring a visual coherence for buses, these public services remain a vital part of London life. Buses carry millions of people to and from work, shopping and entertainment as they have done for decades. Buses are still a major attraction for tourists to the city. We could argue that the New Routemaster already represents the potential future of our road passenger services: there will eventually be at least 800 in use. Alongside the New Routemaster are other more humble vehicles which keep their radical innovations, literally, silent. The hydrogen powered buses on route RV1 point towards future possibilities, as they pass the London Transport Museum where the 'Battle Bus' restoration to working order of centenarian B type bus B2737 has been created to coincide with the commemoration of the First World War in 2014.[10]

This book continues as a social and chronological study of the London bus in all its aspects. The emergence of the horse-drawn bus in London is described by Caroline Warhurst in Chapter 1. Richard Peskett discusses early attempts to replace horse by mechanical propulsion in Chapter 2. Tim Shields describes the B type - the first mass-produced motor bus - in Chapter 3, and Sam Mullins, Director of the London Transport Museum follows it into action along the Western Front during the First World War in Chapter 4. In the return to peace after 1918, London buses developed rapidly, and the London General Omnibus Company succeeded in providing a comprehensive network of services: this is considered by David Lawrence in Chapter 5. For chapter 6, Mike Sutcliffe MBE tells the story of competition between bus operators on London streets in the 1920s. We have seen how London's buses operated on routes into the countryside of Bedfordshire, Berkshire, Buckinghamshire, Essex, Hertfordshire, Kent, Surrey and Sussex. Laurie Akehurst details the now lost Country Bus & Coach network in Chapter 7. In Chapter 8, Simon Murphy reviews the appearance of the bus in popular culture. In Chapter 9 Oliver Green continues the journey through the great period of London Transport expansion in the 1930s, and illustrates how the buses, trams and trolleybuses kept London moving during the Second World War. In chapters 10 and 11, Oliver takes the reader through London Transport's post-war successes and difficulties, noting particularly activities in central London: the innovation of the Routemaster bus, arrival of the first migrant workers, and the 1958 bus strike which would cause lasting problems for the system. With chapters 9, 10 and 11, Oliver Green relates the expansion and development of London Transport road services from the 1930s to the 1950s. In Chapter 12, Roger French examines how the bus competed with the rise of private car ownership during the 1960s, managing a decline in recruitment whilst it helped the New Town developments around London to flourish. This story continues into the 1970s, when the buses faced further decline and ceased to be made in London, for London. In Chapter 13 Roger Torode notes the revival of the London bus, with the Golden Jubilee of London Transport in 1983 and subsequent privatisation of the network. Early trials of 'smart' cashless payment systems are discussed too. To complete this book, Leon Daniels, who has overall responsibility for bus services in the metropolis, reviews the last decade of operations in Chapter 14, and looks ahead to the future for London's buses.

For everyone interested in the heritage of London's buses, the London Transport Museum has many historically important vehicles in its collections, alongside several thousand images and countless artefacts, from tickets and timetables to maps and complete bus stops. Whether hopping from one shop to another along Oxford Street, or travelling back into city life with vintage buses, every journey matters.

The horse bus 1829–1914

Caroline Warhurst

At the beginning of the nineteenth century, London was a compact city of around one million people, where most people walked and journeys on foot were the norm. The streets were narrow and congested and traffic was entirely horse-drawn or hauled by men. It was a city of extremes where the wealthy lived in the West End and used their own carriages, or they hired carriages or cabs, when they needed to travel. The poor meanwhile lived in overcrowded squalor close to where they worked, mostly in the centre. For them the notion of public transport did not exist.

As the city grew, so did the ranks of the middle classes. They began to move out of the centre to live in the pleasanter surroundings of villages and the new suburbs. People still walked into the city to work, or if they could afford it they would book a seat on stage coaches to take them part of the way.

With the population approaching one and a half million, the time was ripe for an entrepreneur to step in and offer a new, more flexible service, with affordable fares. George Shillibeer (1797-1866) launched his Omnibus (meaning 'for all' in Latin) in 1829, after seeing horse bus services operating in Paris. His route ran from Paddington, then at the edge of the city, to the Bank in the City of London. The fare was a shilling. This was expensive, but because the Omnibus stopped at the roadside to take on passengers, unlike the stage coaches, the service was an immediate success. Paddington was also a shrewdly chosen starting point – a popular, growing suburb with the right sort of clientele for Shillibeer's service and far enough outside the centre to guarantee a reliable supply of passengers.

GEORGE SHILLIBEER LAUNCHED HIS OMNIBUS IN 1829

In 1832 the monopoly of the hackney carriages was removed by the Stage Carriage Act, allowing horse buses to operate in the City and pick up passengers for the first time. Within two years there were 376 licensed horse buses in London, in addition to the 423 short stages still operating.[1] With so many competitors and more and more routes opening up Shillibeer was eventually forced out of business. The short stage coaches too had virtually disappeared by 1845, but public transport for ordinary folk had arrived. Vehicle design gradually developed – and the surge in demand created by the Great

Exhibition in 1851 promoted the use of roof seating, to cope with the crowds. Passengers initially sat in a 'back to back' arrangement on the centre of the roof, facing outwards. This 'knifeboard' bus was then superseded in the 1880s by a double deck 'garden seat' vehicle, designed with proper stairs and a platform, and forward-facing roof seats in rows. This became the norm. Passengers knew which horse bus to catch by its colour and name, and the stopping points and destinations painted on the vehicle. As the number of operators grew, some worked cooperatively in 'Associations' to control the number of buses on each route.

In 1856 the London General Omnibus Company (LGOC) started operating. It was originally an Anglo-French enterprise, the Compagnie Generale des Omnibus de Londres. Within a year the company controlled 600 of London's 810 omnibuses and established a consistent level of service for its fleet.[2] It eventually became the largest operator in London and was popularly known as the 'General'. Other large operators included the London Road Car Company and Thomas Tilling & Co.

Despite the coming of the underground railway in 1863 and the arrival of cheaper horse trams running on rails in 1870, the omnibus services continued to successfully target the middle classes in the knowledge they could take them into the West End and the heart of the City, where horse trams were not allowed.

By the 1890s the omnibus catered for a city of around four million people with 2,127 buses on 176 routes using 25,573 horses. Services operated from eight in the morning till late at night. Over the next twenty years however, a revolution was to take place with the development of mechanised vehicles, culminating in the first reliable bus, the B type. When war broke out on 4 August 1914, horses were immediately required for military duties and so ended more than 80 years of the horse bus on London's roads.

Piccadilly Circus in 1891, crowded with horse buses and cabs. Absent from the picture is the famous Shaftesbury Memorial Fountain topped with the winged figure of Anteros - popularly known as Eros - which was not installed until 1893.

1998/44924

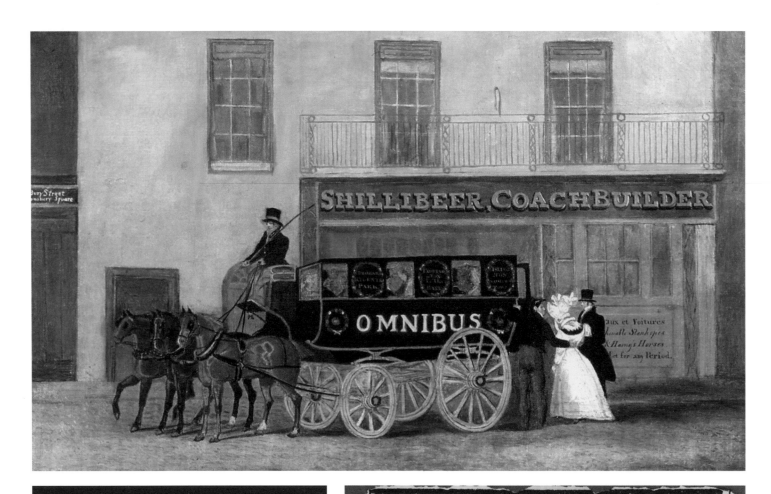

London's first regular bus service was started by George Shillibeer on 4 July 1829. Shillibeer was a coach builder who had seen horse buses operating successfully in Paris and was inspired to begin a similar service in London. The 'Omnibus' ran every three hours with seats for around 20 people sitting round the edge of what was simply a large box on wheels, pulled by three horses. He claimed in his advert that it offered a safer and more comfortable ride than ordinary stage coaches, as all passengers rode inside. The name Omnibus means 'for all' but in reality the fare of one shilling (equivalent to £4 in 2014) was much too expensive for the average London worker. It was however, still less than the price of most short stage coach rides, or cabs.

1996/86
1998/57263

OMNIBUS.

G. SHILLIBEER, induced by the universal admiration the above Vehicles called forth at Paris, has commenced running one upon the Parisian mode, from PADDINGTON to the BANK.

The superiority of this Carriage over the ordinary Stage Coaches, for comfort and safety, must be obvious, all the Passengers being Inside, and the Fare charged from Paddington to the Bank being One Shilling, and from Islington to the Bank or Paddington, only Sixpence.

The Proprietor begs to add, that a person of great respectability attends his Vehicle as Conductor; and every possible attention will be paid to the accommodation of Ladies and Children.

Hours of Starting:—From Paddington Green to the Bank, at 9, 12, 3, 6, and 8 o'clock; from the Bank to Paddington, at 10, 1, 4, 7, and 9 o'clock.

DERRING'S PATENT LIGHT SUMMER

Shillibeer's first route ran from the suburb of Paddington via the 'Angel' public house at Islington and Regent's Park, to Bank in the City; the five mile journey usually took an hour. Shillibeer was originally banned from picking up passengers in central London, an area known as 'the Stones', because the hackney carriages (predecessors of today's taxis) had a monopoly in the area. By 1832 however, pressure from the public and bus operators ended the hackney carriage monopoly and buses were finally allowed to operate in the city centre.

2006/14632

RIVAL OMNIBUSES IN THE YEAR OF QUEEN VICTORIA'S ACCESSION.

London's first omnibus route, 1829

During the 1830s new services sprang up, with rival bus operators competing for passengers, often racing each other to pick up fares. There were no fixed bus stops and passengers could hail a bus from the roadside. To stop the bus, passengers would bang on the roof or pull on reins attached to the driver's arms. Later a bell was introduced. By the 1840s the horse bus had replaced most of the short stage coach operations.

1998/80103
1998/50951

After Shillibeer's large Omnibus, smaller buses came into use carrying 12 passengers in a small box-shaped coach pulled by two horses. An 'improved omnibus' with a raised roof featured in the Illustrated London News 1 May 1847. A larger doorway made it easier for people to board the bus. As competition grew, operators introduced vehicles with lighter frames, like the 'knifeboard' horse bus pictured. It acquired this name because of the seating arrangement on top where passengers, sitting back to back on the long seat, resembled the knifeboards commonly seen in Victorian kitchens. This LGOC horse bus, with the conductor perched on his platform at the back, is in service in 1859 between Putney Bridge and Piccadilly. The knifeboard, London's first double deck bus, remained the standard vehicle during the 1860s and 70s, until replaced by the 'Garden Seat' type in the 1880s.
2004/10874

In the face of increasing competition, George Shillibeer himself went bankrupt. Unable to pay his debts, he was sent to debtors' prison and spent the last years of his life as an undertaker, having adapted his bus for use as a hearse. He died aged 69 in 1866 and is buried in Chigwell in Essex.
1999/20254

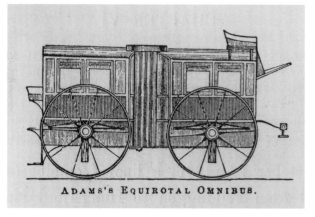

ADAMS'S EQUIROTAL OMNIBUS.

The city's congested narrow streets provided a challenge for omnibus operators, but one inventor came up with a novel design to overcome this. Around 1839, Mr W B Adams constructed a vehicle in two parts, joined in the middle by a flexible leather passage to enable it to turn more easily – the original bendy bus.[4] Sadly it did not become popular and only had a short career.
2006/6166

The Great Exhibition of 1851 in Hyde Park brought a dramatic increase in the number of visitors to London and bus operators were quick to seize the chance to increase the number of passengers carried up to 25, by installing seats on the roof. The exhibition lasted six months and was visited by more than six million people. It was the biggest single tourist attraction London had ever seen. More seats per vehicle led to cheaper fares and the omnibus became even more popular as a form of transport.

2004/18112

Travelling by omnibus in London was not always a pleasant experience. The buses were often crowded, with dirty straw on the floor and journeys were often extremely slow on London's busy streets. In 1833 a reporter in *New Monthly Magazine* remarked 'Here we are ... in all six and twenty sweating citizens, jammed, crammed and squeezed into each other like so many peas in a pod...'. This illustration by William Maw Egley in *The Illustrated London News*, June 1859 also captures the experience. Despite this, by 1860 the LGOC alone was carrying more than 40 million passengers a year, even though it was only the middle classes who could afford to use buses regularly.[6]

1998/99381

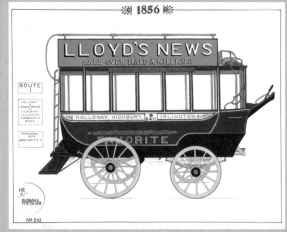

Catching a bus could be complicated. Route numbers were not introduced until 1906, and maps came even later in 1911, so passengers identified the bus they needed by the fleet name, colour, destination and stopping points, displayed on the vehicle. Conveniently though, buses could stop to pick up passengers or set them down anywhere at the roadside. This 1852 painting by James Pollard is of a Favorite horse bus in predominantly green livery at Islington Green. The 'Favorite' fleet run by E & J Wilson of Holloway grew to be the largest in London, with 50 vehicles, 500 horses and 180 staff. It was later taken over by the LGOC. The drawing above is by Herbert Reinohl, one of the brothers who compiled the extensive Reinohl collection.[5]

2004/14908
2003/6755

This set of instructions for passengers published in the *Times*, 30 January 1836, provides an illuminating picture of the 1830s omnibus experience.

2004/18104

OMNIBUS LAW.

1. Keep your feet off the seats.
2. Do not get into a snug corner yourself, and then open the windows to admit a North-wester upon the neck of your neighbour.
3. Have your money ready when you desire to alight. If your time is not valuable, that of others may be.
4. Do not impose on the conductor the necessity of finding you change : he is not a banker.
5. Sit with your limbs straight, and do not with your legs describe an angle of 45, thereby occupying the room of two persons.
6. Do not spit upon the straw. You are not in a hogsty, but in an omnibus, travelling in a country which boasts of its refinement.
7. Behave respectfully to females, and put not an unprotected lass to the blush, because she cannot escape from your brutality.
8. If you bring a dog, let him be small and confined by a string.
9. Do not introduce large parcels—an omnibus is not a van.
10. Reserve bickerings and disputes for the open field. The sound of your own voice may be music to your own ears—not so, perhaps, to those of your companions.
11. If you will broach politics or religion, speak with moderation : all have an equal right to their opinions, and all have an equal right not to have them wantonly shocked.
12. Refrain from affectation and conceited airs. Remember that you are riding a distance for six pence which, if made in a hackney-coach, would cost you as many shillings; and that, should your pride elevate you above plebeian accommodations, your purse should enable you to command aristocratic indulgencies.

Another bus design appeared later in the 1880s called the 'garden seat' bus. This style of vehicle had sets of forward facing wooden seats, proper stairs to the top deck, and a larger platform on the back, making boarding the bus easier and quicker. Women were able to use the stairs and enjoy the view from the top of the bus for the first time. In keeping with Victorian sensibilities, modesty boards were added to hide the ankles of ascending female passengers. Earlier 'outside' seats had open backs, which proved good business for the pickpockets, so slatted backs were installed to frustrate the light-fingered passengers behind. This picture shows a Thomas Tilling garden seat horse bus, c1890.

1998/86825

The role and character of the men who staffed the buses changed a great deal over the years. The hours were long and hard and early conductors in particular had a poor reputation, reflected in the 1830s cartoon showing a reluctant passenger being pushed on the bus, whether he wishes to board or not. Drivers and conductors had to be licensed from 1838 and display their enamel badges. The conductor in the 1890s photograph is also wearing a *Bell Punch* ticket machine and his right hand is grasping the cord, which communicated with the driver. The *Bell Punch* was introduced in 1893 by the LGOC and remained in use into the 1950s.

1998/84021
1998/84378
1991/28
2003/19801

AN EXTENSIVE TAKE IN.

This selection of tickets for the Atlas and Waterloo Omnibus Association is from the Reinohl collection. All the tickets have a hole made by the *Bell Punch*. It was a simple machine, which punched a hole in the ticket once issued, to prevent reuse. As the ticket was cancelled, a small bell would ring and an internal counter recorded it. The punched out circles of coloured paper were retained inside the machine and could be used to check the conductor's takings.

2003/13815

This photograph shows the inside of an unnamed LGOC stable around 1911. Operating horse buses was an expensive business as the horses needed far more care and maintenance than the hardy wooden vehicles they pulled. Each bus required 12 horses to stay on the road. As well as the cost of the horses and the omnibus itself, there were also the costs of stabling, food and vet's fees to take into account. Most horse bus routes started and finished outside pubs, where the animals could be conveniently watered and changed.

1998/85070

The last quarter of the nineteenth century was the heyday of the horse omnibus and this busy view of Fleet Street in the City around 1887 is typical. The Metropolitan Streets Act of 1867 made it a requirement that omnibuses should both travel and stop only on the left hand side of the road (rather than cross the road to pick up or drop passengers, as they did before). As a result horse-bus designs only needed a nearside platform for access, a feature which carried over to the motor buses which followed. In this photo the conductor stands on the platform, keeping his eyes peeled for customers.

1998/89631

This scene at the Bank in the 1880s features one of the original Metropolitan and South Eastern Railway Knifeboard omnibuses, which began operating in 1866, three years after the underground railway opened. The fare charged for this service which ran between the various railway stations was one old penny. The Metropolitan was particularly distinctive with its huge red umbrella, which both sheltered the driver and helped identify the bus.

1998/89838

When horse trams began operating in 1870 they presented a significant threat to the horse omnibus. Because they ran on rails and could carry more passengers, fares were cheaper. Electrification around 1900 increased the popularity of trams and contributed to the decline of the horse bus, although in the areas where trams were not allowed, the horse still held prime position for a while longer. In this 1890s picture taken at the Plough Inn, Clapham Common, a crowded Stephenson horse tram, operating between Tooting and Waterloo Station, passes a stationary garden seat horse bus.

1998/83567

Here we see the last LGOC horse bus leaving London Bridge station on 25 October 1911. In 1900 London's transport was still dependent on horse power but running costs were high and bus operators struggled with competition from the Underground and trams. Electricity had also arrived as an alternative source of power. When the LGOC introduced the purpose-built B type bus in 1910, it signalled the end for the horse bus and within a year the last LGOC horse bus was withdrawn. The last horse bus, operated by Thomas Tilling, was withdrawn from service on the evening of 4th August 1914, the day the First World War was declared.

1999/20636

First generation buses

Richard Peskett

At the start of the 1890s, Victoria was still Queen and talk of the Boer War had yet to be the topic of conversation. Already Britain was becoming a very mobile nation, and the invention of the motor car and the use of the internal combustion engine, was about to change for ever the way of life in the last decade of the 19th century. Mechanically powered road vehicles in the form of steam carriages began services in London in the 1830s. Walter Hancock of Stratford operated his 'Era', 'Autopsy' and 'Automation' steam carriages. On its first journey from Moorfields to Paddington in 1834, 'Era' achieved a reported average speed of 12 miles per hour. The 22-seat 'Automation' ran with reasonable success until 1840. Ultimately, the logistics of operation defeated these first generation motorised vehicles. Consequently, the horse-drawn bus and tram were to reign supreme for another five decades.

Development in continental Europe, along with the Road Traffic Act of 1896 in favour of mechanical power, brought about the reality of the motor bus. Prospectuses for investment in this novel mode of transport soon appeared. Many were ebullient and optimistic, unsound or even fraudulent, promising speculators large fleets of vehicles and vast financial returns. People were now travelling greater distances to their workplace and required better forms of transport. There were odd attempts with steam and electric traction in this pioneering period, but the first recognisable motor bus appeared in April 1898. It was followed by two new vehicles, built in Bristol and fitted with German Daimler engines. Finally entering service in October 1899, these should be considered to be the first 'regular' motor buses operating in London. They survived until December 1900, but again operating costs and logistics defeated them. Numerous small wagonettes seating up to 12 people also appeared on the streets but made no real impact on the travelling public.

THE FIRST RECOGNISABLE MOTOR BUS APPEARED IN 1898

From 1904 the situation changed rapidly. The London Road Car Company and the London General Omnibus Company (LGOC) were the two largest horse bus operators, and in 1904 made their debut with motor buses. Thomas Tilling also entered the arena in September with his 34 seat double deck Milnes-Daimler buses operating from Peckham to Oxford Circus. Popular vehicle types during this pioneering era were Milnes-Daimler, De Dion and Straker-Squire. By 1908 these manufacturers accounted for 90% of the market. Attracted by the business prospects, many other operators appeared, but they were beleaguered with mechanical problems which gave rise to serious cost implications, leading to the financial collapse of companies, and a glut of surplus omnibuses on the market.

The London Electrobus Company made a grand entrance and financial flotation using battery-powered electric vehicles. But with far less vehicles being purchased than had been intended the whole operation was considered by many to be fraudulent. Once again, financial collapse followed.

Gradually, the LGOC acquired the vehicles and operating interests of virtually all other companies, except Thomas Tilling with whom the LGOC would join forces at a later date. In acquiring the Vanguard Motorbus Company in July 1908 an engineering base workshop at Walthamstow was obtained. The Vanguard and its constituent companies had realised as early as 1906 the problems with operating 'off the shelf' buses and had been actively working on vehicles designed especially for London use.

Scotland Yard had always been a thorn in the side of the operators, all vehicles having to be inspected before being licenced. New regulations were issued in March 1909 that all vehicles would have to be under 3 ton 10 cwt unladen weight. So the LGOC, having inherited many problems, decided to set about designing a completely new vehicle for London use. This vehicle incorporated the better features from operational experience gained from some 28 different vehicles. The result was a 34 seat double deck bus to be known as the X type of which 61 were produced. This was soon to be succeeded by the B type and it heralded the beginning of a new era of vehicles constructed specifically for London use and an operational policy destined to last some five decades.

The new and the old at Charing Cross in February 1900. The first 'regular' motor bus service opened on 9 October 1899 from Kennington to Victoria via Westminster. It was operated by the Motor Traction Company and run by Percy Frost-Smith. Seating was for 12 inside and 14 outside, the fare being 2d for the entire distance and 1d for intermediate stages. Built by Owen, Brazil and Holborow at Bristol it was fitted with a 4 cylinder German Daimler engine. Giving the public the first experience of motor bus travel this truly was the dawn of a new era. There is no doubt that the 2d was well spent. The service lasted until December 1900.

1998/75518.

The Canstatt-built Daimler is considered to be the first London motor bus of practical build. Fitted with a two cylinder 14 horse power engine and of typical continental appearance, it was imported by the British Motor Car Company in March 1898. It is in the workshop of E H Bayley, Newington Causeway, about to be fitted with a more conventional double deck horse bus style of body. Exhibited at various shows around London, including an appearance at the 'Omnibus Meeting' on the Embankment of June 1898, it saw little or no public service but provided much useful operational knowledge. The 'Steam Omnibus Company Limited' was part of a grand scheme, which ultimately failed to put 100 steam buses into service.

Richard Peskett collection

Walter Flexman French formed the South Western Motor Car Company, and was later involved in several pioneering provincial bus businesses. French used these Coventry-built Daimler and MMC wagonettes for an inaugural trip between Balham and Staines in March 1901. The following month they began regular service between Streatham and Clapham Junction. Owing to the vehicles' inability to climb the incline on Tooting Common when fully loaded, the service was curtailed to the 'Wheatsheaf', Tooting, but maintenance costs soon saw the service withdrawn altogether. Similar vehicles carrying 8 passengers were used by Francis Bell for a Piccadilly to Putney service opened in September 1901, and there were at least 40 other licenced operators of wagonettes. Bell enjoyed a little more success than French, but by 1903 the era of the wagonette was over.

Richard Peskett collection

The London Road Car Company was the first of the old horse bus companies to experiment with steam traction. This innovative Thornycroft, coal-fired and with a water tube type steam wagon boiler, was fitted with an adapted horse bus body. Its canopy, an unusual nod to passenger comfort for the period, afforded little protection from smoke and sparks. Seating 36 people, it entered service in March 1902 between Hammersmith and Oxford Circus via Shepherds Bush. This steam bus was acclaimed as manageable and of reasonable speed but un-wieldy and ugly: the service only ran for two months, and was withdrawn as uneconomic. The vehicle was exported to South Africa and reported by *Commercial Motor* as 'still working at Port Elizabeth, South Africa', in January 1909.

1998/75354

Purporting to be the first large double deck omnibus running on rubber, rather than steel, tyres, this Canstatt-built Daimler had a 4-cylinder engine and hot tube ignition. Bodywork was designed by pioneer motorist and entrepreneurial businessman Harry Lawson. Much involved with the supply of motor vehicles, Lawson was part organiser and competitor in the 'emancipation' run to Brighton in 1896. Seating 12 inside and 15 out this Daimler was placed in service by Claude Dennis in October 1902. Operating between Lewisham, Lee Green and Eltham in south east London, this heavy and cumbersome looking vehicle managed to survive until early 1904.

1998/88976

Steam as a form of motive power was important to early motor bus operators. Both the London Road Car and the London General Omnibus (LGOC) companies purchased Thomas Clarkson-built steam buses in 1904–05. Referred to as 'Chelmsford's' after the town where they were produced, Clarkson buses used paraffin as fuel. They were relatively easy to operate and with the driver in a high and commanding position, the vehicle was no doubt driven with considerable gusto. Frank Searle, chief engineer of the LGOC, expressed his own enthusiasm in 1908: 'Mr. Searle holds steadfastly to the opinion that he can secure solid advantages by the employment of steamers and is by no means enamoured of the petrol propelled vehicles for London omnibus work'. Clarkson was later to form the National Steam Car Company, which took over the Chelmsford factory and operated an extensive vehicle fleet in London.

Richard Peskett collection

The third year of successful Public Service in England.

These Cars have no Change Gears and no Clutch.

They have Direct Drive at all Speeds, hence the characteristic smooth and swift movement.

Paraffin Fuel is used.

CLARKSON LTD., Chelmsford.

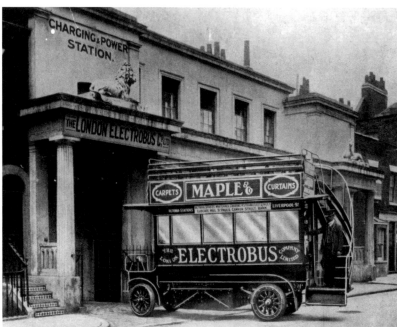

Registered and with a capital of £305,000, the London Electrobus Company (LEC) started services in 1907 using the then cutting edge technology of battery powered vehicles. This is their charging and power station. Buses were assembled at West Norwood, south London, and were to comprise an eventual fleet of 300. Only 20 were purchased by the LEC, however, and the organisation received much criticism in the trade and financial press relating to alleged misrepresentation, and fraudulent activity. Offers to return shareholders' money were made and a High Court action occurred. The company managed to stay in business for four years, attempting in this period to fit a top canopy to the buses: this was refused under Metropolitan Police regulations for motor vehicles. The final passing of the company in 1910 went virtually unnoticed, with at least 12 of the redundant buses finding further use in Brighton.

1998/77517

With the advent of motor traction new opportunities arose for the tourist industry. The Great Western Railway soon took advantage of this by running sightseeing trips from Paddington station. In 1908 another service began from Adam Street, Strand, using three electric vehicles and two Wolseley-Siddley charabancs. The electric vehicles were similar to those already working in New York and were imported from the Vehicle Equipment Company in that city. *Motor Traction* of June 1908 suggested that the service would struggle to survive in competition with the cheap motor bus fares then available. This seems not to be an issue for the tourist sightseeing buses presently operating in London.

Richard Peskett collection

"Seeing London"

AUTOMOBILES

LEAVE

BOOKING OFFICE

AND

WAITING ROOM,

ADAM STREET,

STRAND;

(Near Hotel Cecil)

DAILY

10 A.M. AND 2 P.M.

HAMPTON COURT

SUNDAYS 11 A.M.

Built by Brush at Loughborough - more renowned for tramcar construction of the day - this is one of seven similar vehicles operated from 1906–1908 by the Amalgamated Motor Bus Company. Like many of its peers, Amalgamated expressed intentions to put over 100 buses on the road, but this plan came to nothing. The design of driver over engine and a claim that the first 'all metal' body was used are of note. The history of Amalgamated is intriguing: involving the British Automobile Development Company, it became the British Electric Traction Company in 1910, forming the foundation of the business that would own one of the largest share holdings in British bus operation for the next six decades.

1998/89282

The London Motor Omnibus Company was the first to promote long distance travel to the south coast. Their inaugural run to Brighton took place on 30 August 1905 using a Milnes-Daimler double-decker (a single deck vehicle with heating was used in the winter months). Leaving the Hotel Victoria in Northumberland Avenue, near Trafalgar Square at 9am, and returning from Brighton at 4pm, the round trip of 100 miles cost a return fare of 7 shillings and 6 pence (equivalent to around £35 today). The first run had an unforeseen delay of one hour at Redhill when it was found out that an additional licence to pick up passengers or ply for hire, was required in the county of Surrey. The service enjoyed reasonable success for almost 12 months.

1998/69956

The London Motor Omnibus Company's daily service to Brighton ran well until disaster struck on 12 July 1906. A vehicle on a private hire job, carrying mainly tradesmen from the Orpington area to Brighton, suffered a major mechanical failure in the transmission resulting in very little braking power. It ran out of control soon after starting the hill descent south of Handcross on the Brighton road. The driver attempted to stop the bus by running it against a bank, but this failed. Most of the bodywork was destroyed by an overhanging branch, 10 passengers were killed and many others seriously injured. The remains of the bus were pulled back onto the road by a steam traction engine.

2004/14230

Handcross Hill, The Wrecked "Vanguard"

The "Scott-Stirling"—"The Omnibus de Luxe."

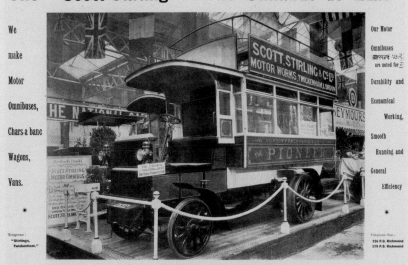

We make Motor Omnibuses, Chars-a banc Wagons, Vans.

*

Telegrams :
"Stirlings,
Twickenham."

SCOTT. STIRLING & Co. Ltd.
MOTOR WORKS, TWICKENHAM, LONDON.

Our Motor Omnibuses are noted for Durability and Economical Working, Smooth Running and General Efficiency

*

Telephone Nos :
236 P.O. Richmond
579 P.O. Richmond

"Scott-Stirling" 24-30 h.p. Omnibus.

Its wearing qualities are unsurpassed and for smooth and quiet running it is unrivalled.

With the trading name 'Pioneer', the London Power Omnibus Company commenced operations in 1902 with a small Scott-Sterling single deck omnibus, plying between Cricklewood and Oxford Circus. The manufacturer made much of the fact that the vehicle was of all-British build, in an attempt to lure buyers from a market almost entirely dominated by continental makes. To accommodate its rapidly expanding fleet – there were some 50 buses on the road by early 1907 – a large garage was opened at Cricklewood. This ambition was not to last: disputes with manufacturer Scott-Sterling brought an early end to operations, with liquidation taking place in July 1907. *Motor Traction* magazine for 26 October reported that the entire fleet and operation was offered for sale by public auction. There were several similar situations in the infant motor bus industry, and a glut of second hand vehicles made sales difficult. With bidding only reaching £23,000, the reserve was not met and the business was withdrawn from auction.

Richard Peskett collection

The London Power Omnibus Company made a serious effort with the training of staff, and shown here are a group of would be drivers and mechanics at their Cricklewood depot in 1907 with their 'training' chassis. *Motor Traction* for August 1907 reported that a question had been asked in the Houses of Parliament regarding noise and discomforts to residents made by motor buses changing gears around Piccadilly and surrounding streets. The reply was that 'all drivers are tested as to their capacity to change gear without undue noise'.

1998/88979

Once Thomas Clarkson decided the best future for his business lay in both the building and operation of steam-powered buses, he assembled chassis at Chelmsford, and brought bodies some considerable distance from Hurst Neilson at Motherwell, Lanarkshire. Using paraffin as fuel, Clarkson's vehicles were reliable and gave good service for a decade from 1909 with the fleet name National Steam Car Company. Services ran in London, with some 173 buses in use at the peak, but in 1919 an arrangement with the London General saw the last one withdrawn.

Richard Peskett collection

Vehicles operating in London were subject to harsh road conditions. *Motor Traction* of November 1907 reported: 'Surely it is time for London local authorities to clean the streets, at times it is almost impossible for motor 'buses to proceed at all because of all the thick grease'. Cobble or wood block paving became very slippery and much damage was done to wheels as the rear of vehicles slid on the camber of the road and struck the kerb. To maintain buses, they received a heavy overhaul on an annual basis, this taking place in their operational garage. This is Mortlake Garage, around 1908 ,with DeDion chassis in view and smartly turned out staff.

1998/63370

Postcard cartoon of a grossly overloaded 'Vanguard' Milnes-Daimler. Posted in August 1906, the sender has written: 'how would you like to be on this bus. It looks like one could have quite a nice time doesn't it? Have a good look and find out all the different items thereon – I know the originator'. Postcards were an important means of communication at this time.

Richard Peskett collection

A political cartoon of the Edwardian period: this postcard image is undoubtedly of a London motor bus, at the time when maintenance costs were causing serious problems with the finances of their operators.

Richard Peskett collection

One of the large fleet of Milnes-Daimlers operated by the London Motor Omnibus Company under the 'Vanguard' fleet name. With bodywork built by the United Electric Car Company of Preston, these vehicles gave reasonably reliable service. This image of 1907 is from a contemporary postcard, and would have been hand tinted to give the coloured effect. Much revenue was obtained by the operators from advertising theatre productions of the day.

Richard Peskett collection

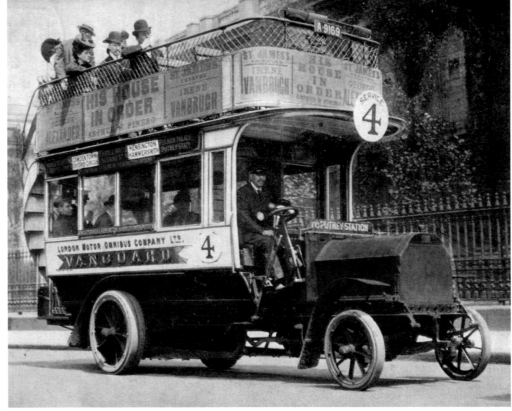

The firm of Sidney Straker and Squire arranged to sell the German built Bussing chassis in Britain from about 1904. The LGOC was a very good customer, and this was one of its first such vehicles to enter service in May 1905. By 1906 Straker and Squire were building their own chassis of similar design, many of which were fitted with Wolseley engines. By 1908 there were over 250 Straker-Squires running in London. Hengler's Italian Circus was one of the popular entertainments of the day.

Richard Peskett collection

Driving a bus was hard work around 1906. Milnes-Daimler buses, such as this one operated by Thomas Tilling, afforded little in the way of protection from the weather, winter or summer. Starting the motor required a strong arm to turn the handle in front of the radiator. The cobble sets forming the road surface were treacherous when wet. Managing the bus passengers, the conductor is smartly dressed with waistcoat and bowler hat. Tillings had been in business for many years as horse bus operators and without doubt this crew had started in that era. The illuminated destination indicator was an new innovation at this time.

1998/88787

The popularity of riding on the upper deck can be clearly seen with this Great Eastern London Motor Omnibus Company's Guildford-built Dennis. They were keen to advertise their route bringing in passengers from Upton Park, home of the recently formed West Ham Football Club, through the heart of the East End to the different world of the Oxford Street and the central area. The company managed to survive better than most, and it was not until 1911 that it became part of the LGOC.

1998/89123

Little other mechanical transport is visible as this Straker-Squire gets under way from the kerb and passes a De Dion both in the ownership of the London General. This is summer time 1907 with men in straw boaters and ladies wearing large hats enjoying the ride on the top deck. Nestle's Milk and Hudsons Soap were popular consumables of the day and both took out extensive advertising on the omnibuses. Within another four years the LGOC horse bus was to move into the annals of history but horses were to remain popular for the transport of commercial goods for many more years to come.

1998/83691

The London & District Motor 'Bus Company commenced trading in October 1905 with this Straker-Squire or Bussing. The fleet name of 'White Arrow' was rapidly changed to 'Arrow'. The ornate style of signwriting, all executed by hand, was one widely used for omnibuses of the period. Like many of their contemporaries, the London and District experienced financial difficulties, and by mid-1907 had joined forces with three other operators to form the London Motor Omnibus Company, with a combined fleet of over 420 vehicles.

1998/89126

The London & Provincial Motor Bus & Traction Company Limited - a grand title in the public's eye, operated under the 'Arrow' fleet name and had a arrow pointer mounted on the roof above the driver. This French built *Lacoste et Battman* would have seated 16 persons inside on upholstered seating and a further 18 on wooden seats exposed to the elements on the top deck. Driver, conductor and inspector are smartly turned out in proper uniforms with the driver wearing riding boots, a legacy from horse bus days.

1998/89137

Following the acquisition of the Walthamstow workshops in 1908, the LGOC introduced the first purpose-built London bus as the X type. After testing from August 1909, it entered public service in December of the same year. The initial production batch of 61 vehicles still met with objections from the Metropolitan Police on the grounds of noise. The testing ground was Wimbledon Common, south west London, known to the men as 'Siberia', no doubt a cold and bleak spot on winter days. With noise problems eventually overcome, the X type proved to be a sound reliable design which would give rise to the world's first mass production motor omnibus chassis: the B type. X35 is well laden with school children, excited by the prospect of a day out by motor bus.

1999/20100

A Bird's Eye View of Walthamstow Works of Associated Equipment Co.
Part enclosed in white line shows extent of Works in 1906.

Included in the assets of the Vanguard Motorbus Company acquired by the LGOC in July 1908, were their workshops and engineering base at Walthamstow. This facility reflected the previous owner's realisation that vehicles had to be specially designed and built for the rigours of London use. Under LGOC control, a programme of development was immediately pursued at Walthamstow, resulting in the construction of an entirely new generation of passenger vehicles which were much quieter and more reliable. Revised Metropolitan Police regulations introduced in 1909, had to be incorporated – seating was still restricted to 16 inside and 18 on top. Such was the success of the Walthamstow Works, by 1921 it had been substantially extended.

Richard Peskett collection

'How to recognise the Motor Buses of To-day'. The Clarkson steam bus and Orion bus published in *Automotor Journal* September 1906.

Richard Peskett collection

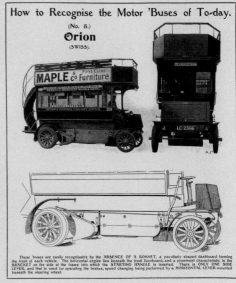

A cartoon from *Commercial Motor* magazine 21 September 1905, showing another of the difficulties experienced by operators of motorised transport. This London Motor Omnibus Company 'Vanguard' bus has been caught on the Brighton road in a 'speed trap'. Such traps, set by a hidden team of police, aimed to catch, and profit from fining vehicles exceeding the antiquated speed limits. On the right, the figure of justice is drawn blindfolded.

Richard Peskett collection

THE SPIRIT OF THE LAW PUTS THE
DRAG ON ENTERPRISE.

A fine of £10 and costs was recently imposed upon the driver for an alleged speed of 32 miles an hour. Passengers voluntarily came forward to deny that the bus "rocked and swayed" or that it was being driven at a high speed.

The B type bus, 1910–14

Tim Shields

On the evening of 25 October 1911 the last horse bus belonging to the London General Omnibus Company (LGOC) pulled away from Moorgate Street.[1] A camera flashed as the packed Service 32 trotted off towards London Bridge and a once familiar sight faded into history. The LGOC transformation to motor-bus operation was complete. London's bus users had become increasingly accustomed to the sound and smell of the petrol engine over previous years, with 863 motor buses in service by 1910.[2] It was the introduction of one particular design of bus, that would enable rapid withdrawal of the remaining horse fleet and the beginning of a new era.

Through operating a mixture of 28 different types of early motor buses built by numerous manufacturers, the LGOC recognised the need for a standardised vehicle that would be both reliable and efficient. Under the guidance of Frank Searle, Chief Motor Engineer, the company confidently set out to design and build its own. The first attempt, designated the X type, incorporated the best technological features then available, including a lightweight chassis and worm-driven rear axle. Striving for further improvements to the engine, gearbox and transmission, this quickly led to the development of the B type bus.

The first British commercial vehicle built using the production line techniques pioneered by Henry Ford for motor car manufacture, the B type was constructed from parts made to such fine measurements that many components were interchangeable. This made the fleet reliable, easier and cheaper to maintain. LGOC engineers tried to meet the needs of their colleagues in the commercial department, who were calling for bigger and faster buses. Industrial innovation could provide solutions, but it was constrained by Metropolitan Police regulations which reflected a cautious official approach to vehicle weight and size based on fears of traffic accidents and damage to road surfaces. Consequently the B type was limited to an unladen weight to 3.5 tons, a capacity of 34 passengers and a top speed of 12 mph. However, such was its success, within two years of its introduction, the Associated Equipment company's factory in Walthamstow was employing 1,700 people, building B type buses at a rate of 30 per week.[3]

WITHIN TWO YEARS, 30 B TYPES WERE BEING BUILT EACH WEEK

Liberated by a dependable fleet of motor buses, routes expanded to serve districts and suburbs springing up around London. New patterns of commuting emerged as districts poorly served by Tube, rail or tramcar were linked up for the first time. Promoting bus travel for leisure, several routes extended even further, linking the town pavement with the countryside hedgerow beyond. From 1911, bus maps showed the growth of routes: 23 on the first map, and more than a hundred by spring 1914. By 1913 there were 2,500 B type buses in service, each carrying on average 340,000 passengers annually along 600 miles of roads. Integration of LGOC bus services advanced significantly in January 1912, when the company became part of the Underground Group, operator of several deep tube and sub-surface railways. Now, propelled by the extraordinary management vision of Albert Stanley and Frank Pick, combined road and rail facilities and publicity could better serve the travelling public in Edwardian London.

B type buses in the City of London at the Bank of England during the First World War. The banner displayed on the front of the Royal Exchange building reads 'Let London lead! Buy your National War Bonds now', 1917.

1998/85602

The LGOC's winged wheel design –
origin of Transport for London's roundel
symbol - was carried on buses from
1905 to 1912, when it was dropped in
favour of the more succinct 'GENERAL'
fleet name. It remained in use for staff
uniforms for some years, and is seen
worn by Driver Reuben H Collins in a
posed photograph with his daughter,
about 1920.

2007/3873

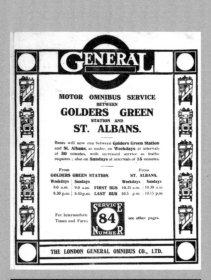

The first streamlined version
manifestation of the roundel, was on
this publicity leaflet for LGOC route 84,
Golder's Green to St. Albans, of 1912.

David Lawrence collection

The B type bus worked in the teeming streets of the city, and far out into London's countryside. This poster produced in 1914, 'The Open Road - Fresh Air and Sunshine', by Walter Spradbery, conveys the optimism and enterprise of the age in which the B type was developed.

2000/9529

THE OPEN ROAD
FRESH AIR AND SUNSHINE

The basic seating arrangement of the B type was little different from the Victorian horse bus. Whilst the upper-deck was popular with passengers, particularly smokers or people seeking fresh air during warm and dry weather, little protection was offered. In an attempt to improve comfort in bleak conditions, canvas seat covers were trialled and fitted, with limited success.

1998/87761
2004/16204
1998/39935

The rise of motor traffic led to an unprecedented rise in accidents, as passengers and pedestrians unaccustomed to higher vehicle speeds, acceleration and braking, misjudged their movements. To reduce the risk of injury, the LGOC embarked on a public safety initiative. Introduced in the 1910s, the 'Safety First' campaign used leaflets, posters, signs and short films played in cinema halls, to explain the correct behaviour for pedestrians when around the faster-moving motor buses.

2000/3632
2005/1110
1998/83844

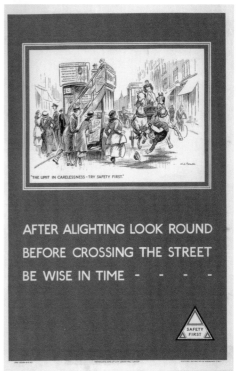

Running between Cricklewood and
Liverpool Street, route 94 was the first
to introduce motor bus operation during
the night. Providing a service popular
with late-shift workers, B185 is seen in
the early hours of the morning outside
Piccadilly Circus Underground station.
1998/85474

On a wet and dreary afternoon in 1918 pedestrians and road traffic slowly make their way across a heavily congested London Bridge. During the morning and evening rush hour, river crossings became thoroughfare pinch points as commuters and vehicles jostled for space.

1998/85329

Despite the rain, a few brave people can be seen on the open top deck of B568 as it makes its way on route 4 along New Bridge Street in the City of London, towards Bermondsey, c1920. Many goods haulage vehicles remained horse-drawn until motor vehicles became cheaper to run, and could be relied upon not to break down in service.

1998/87596

Greenland Street, Camden Town in 1920. Day trippers on the upper deck eagerly await departure for Reigate. With a top speed of 12mph, it took a demanding 2½ hours for the bus to reach the historic market town some 25 miles away.

1998/43717

To close this chapter, as war approached in August 1914, we see the poster paired to the one with which we started the story of the B type. In Walter Spradbery's 'The Homeward Way In The Cool Of Day', our Reigate day trippers return to London at dusk.

1983/4/549

THE HOMEWARD WAY
IN THE COOL OF DAY

TRY A TRIP
ON ROUTE
160 REIGATE.
DAILY FROM
STOCKWELL STATION.

4

The B type bus and the First World War

Sam Mullins

The cheering crowds that thronged Whitehall, Trafalgar Square and the Strand to welcome the declaration of war on Germany at midnight on 4 August 1914 expected the conflict to be short and victorious. Bus drivers whose buses were stuck in the crowds, and from which revellers had a grandstand view of the celebrations, had little idea that they might find both themselves and their buses on the Western Front within a matter of weeks. Certainly, the duration and profound effect of war on the London of 1914, and on its transport staff and vehicles, could hardly have been anticipated.

London was on the doorstep of the conflict; the city was a hive of activity for five years, the centre for wartime operations which brought civilians and the armed services into common cause. Stations in the metropolis were thronged with soldiers and sailors departing for the fighting fronts or returning on leave, and arriving wounded destined for the capital's many hospitals. Most munitions were manufactured around London and transported with food and fodder, guns and equipment, horses, vehicles and medical supplies, via the capital, to France and beyond.

With insufficient motor vehicles of its own, the British Army requisitioned over one thousand buses (about one third of the London bus fleet). These were sent to France, accompanied by their drivers, who were recruited into the Army Service Corps (ASC). A touch of London was brought to the battlefields, as convoys of buses, initially with their bright red livery, adverts and route boards intact, carried troops into the front line and brought the wounded out. From January 1915 a former workhouse at Grove Park, south London, became the ASC centre for training staff and converting buses.

A major social issue in the years before the war had been the emancipation of women. As the armed services consumed more and more men, they were for the first time 'substituted' by women on the home front. Many women who had previously been largely unseen as domestic servants, now became highly visible as bus conductors, platform staff, railway guards, cleaners and lift attendants. This emancipation of

women was significantly advanced, despite their being displaced by the return of men from the forces. In 1918, 8.4 million women, aged 28 and over, gained the vote. Post war London was much changed; it had lost many men, was wracked by the influenza epidemic of 1919/20 and its economy, disrupted by four years of war. The shortage of buses led to reduced services in London and standing on the lower deck was

THE B TYPE BROUGHT A TOUCH OF LONDON TO THE BATTLEFIELDS

permitted from 1916 as a result. Transport struggled to return to normal with khaki lorry buses drafted onto the capital's streets. A handful of buses returned to London service and one, B43, was presented to George V and rechristened Ole Bill after Bruce Bairnsfather's wartime cartoon character. Veteran bus drivers were the only civilians to march in the first Armistice Day parade in 1920, accompanied by Ole Bill as a mobile memorial to the busmen's contribution to the war effort. Memorials to the fallen were placed in London's bus garages, on railway stations and in every parish church.

The early weeks of the war were characterised by patriotic fervour among many Londoners, resulting in a clamour to enlist in the services. Here a B type bus carries City of London Police volunteers to a recruiting station near George Street, 1914. Recruiting posters have been pinned on the front of the bus and a large crowd of bowler-hatted City workers have turned out to join with the volunteers' enthusiasm.

1998/36810

Daimler bus D70 carrying troops in Ghent, October 1914. The first London buses to go to war were deployed rapidly; keeping their blue London MET (Metropolitan Electric Tramways) livery and even their adverts. In the initial mobile phase of the war, they were used to rescue soldiers and civilians from the invading German Army during the siege of Antwerp. This bus carries wounded soldiers and is passing a private car marked with a red cross. The Daimler sleeve-valve engine is making its characteristic exhaust smoke.

1998/84914

On this postcard, Instructors are pictured on war service at Osterley Park, west London, c1916. Training of drivers also took place at the army camp at Osterley Park. This group of instructors is from the General and many wear the summer uniform of a white duster coat.

Michael Young collection

Army Service Corps, Motor Transport, Grove Park, c1914–15. There were no garage facilities at Grove Park, south London, where buses and their crews were prepared for war service. Here buses are lined up in nearby Chinbrook Road, where they are being painted khaki before going to France. There is even a large tin of paint next to the rear wheel of the bus on the left of the postcard.

Michael Young collection

Postcard, 'La Guerre dans le Nord – les autobus de Londres', 1916. A large convoy of buses with troops on board in the main square at Bethune, northern France, much of which was destroyed in 1918. Bethune was behind the allied lines for much of the war, a place where soldiers were brought to relax away from the front line. Large convoys of seventy or eighty vehicles were used, working only by night near the Front to avoid being observed and shelled.

2014/178

Walking wounded board a London bus on the Western Front. With a thin layer of snow on the ground, the walking wounded are being loaded onto a bus, now lacking its mudguards and with its glass windows painted over. Two officers are in discussion in the foreground.

1998/38988

Troops 'embussing' on the Western Front, c1914. A division of 20,000 men could be loaded onto a column of buses in about thirty minutes, enabling the army to respond quickly and move men where they were needed. Here in a tree lined street, soldiers with heavy packs and blanket rolls have climbed up the stairs, used by civilians in London only a few weeks before. Note the water can by the top step and the light once used to illuminate the rear destination board.
1998/39220

Many buses had their bodies removed and were converted into lorries and over 8,000 B type chassis for lorries were built by the AEC at Walthamstow. Six B types were converted into mobile pigeon lofts. Homing pigeons were a reliable means of communication, released from battle areas to their home lofts in rear areas with messages for HQ. Here B2132 with its crew pose for an official photograph with their bus.
1999/2005

This LGOC poster attracted 20,000 applicants when published in March 1916. Nearly half of those employed as conductors had previously worked as domestic servants. As conductors, these women welcomed the predictable hours, greater responsibility and financial independence. Over the next three years, the LGOC employed some 3,500 women.

2003/24157

LONDON GENERAL OMNIBUS COMPANY, L^{TD.}

WANTED

WOMEN CONDUCTORS

HEIGHT MUST NOT BE LESS THAN 5 FEET AGE BETWEEN 21 AND 35

APPLY BETWEEN 10.0 A.M. AND 1.0 P.M. ON WEEKDAYS (SATURDAYS EXCEPTED)

THE SUPERINTENDENT OF EMPLOYMENT, L.G.O. CO'S. TRAINING SCHOOL, MILMAN'S STREET, S.W.

Women form a long line at the LGOC's training school at Milman's Street, Chelsea, in 1916 to apply for jobs newly available for them. Later that year, LGOC produced an album of photographs recording female recruitment and training to mark the 2,000th woman 'substitute' employed.

1998/48277

Staged photograph of classroom training for new female LGOC bus conductors in 1916. The instructor is pointing at an enlarged Bell Punch bus ticket to explain the fare stages. On the wall behind the women are maps and safety instructions. Before being accepted for training, women had to pass IQ and medical tests and show they had no criminal record.

1998/39914

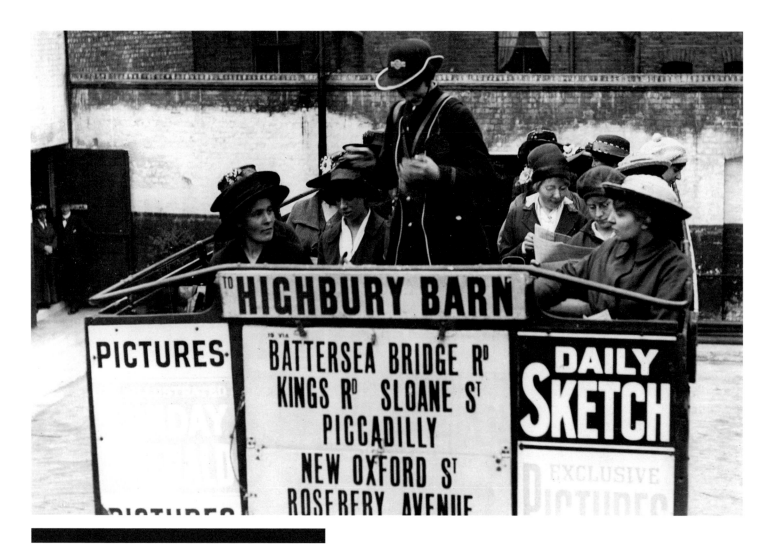

A new female conductor tries out her recently-acquired skills on a group of 'passengers' on top of a bus in the yard at the Milmans Street training school. George Savidge was the Conductors' Lecturer from 1912 and taught at Milmans Street, which opened in 1913. He said in 1937, 'Wearing the uniform week in and week out got too monotonous for some of them. One effected a change by cutting off the tunic collar, making a V-shaped front and trimming the edges with pink chiffon; another tilted up one side of her broad brimmed hat and sewed a bunch of red artificial roses to the side; whilst yet another cut a hole through the side of her hat and attached an Australian soldier's cockade.'

1998/91203

Remarkably, after the First World War 234 buses were returned to the LGOC by the War Department and over forty were put back into service. Here a B type chassis is being repaired after being brought back from the Western Front in 1919.

1998/36587

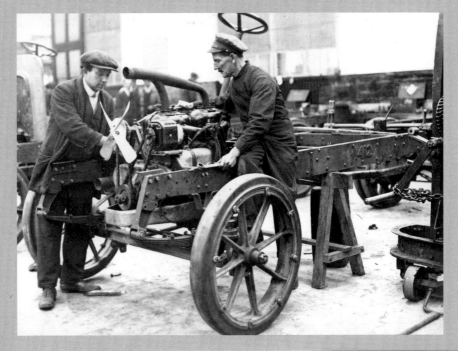

Post-war bus shortages meant that vehicles which would otherwise have been considered substandard, were pressed into use to maintain services in the capital. From May 1919 some returned B type chassis were fitted with very basic wooden 'lorry-bus' bodies, and operated as 'Traffic Emergency Vehicles' in khaki livery, with a fixed wooden staircase built onto the rear tailgate. They were unpopular and, licensed to carry just 27 people with no standing allowed, operated at a loss. This lorry-bus is picking up passengers at Victoria station in 1919.

1998/85345

Many local war memorials for fallen comrades were created at local garages and offices. Here, at the LGOC's Willesden Garage a memorial to the 55 employees who were killed during the war - including one lost during a Zeppelin raid - is being dedicated in November 1920.

1998/43613

B type B43 was invited to visit Buckingham Palace in February 1920, when the bus and 25 veteran busmen were presented to King George V. The King commented that this was the first time he had stepped on to a bus and suggested the men and their bus join the Remembrance parade being planned around the new Cenotaph in November. The bus was later fitted with a radiator cap based on Bruce Bairnsfather's 'Ole Bill character, and an engraved shell casing and plaques, effectively creating a mobile war memorial. The Ole Bill bus and veteran drivers appeared in the London Remembrance Parade annually, and Transport for London staff continue this tradition today.

1998/64651
1998/13714

Driver Tarrant and Conductor Rogers were killed on 8 September 1915 when their bus B804 was hit during a Zeppelin aerial bombing raid while operating on route 8. Their funeral on 20 October 1915 was a major event, after which a set of commemorative photo postcards was issued. The cortege was led through Dalston by wreathed B type buses, and attended by a large contingent of LGOC staff wearing white summer coats with black armbands. The bus on which they died was repaired and put back into service.

1983/191/1
1998/33334

FUNERAL OF VICTIMS OF AIR RAID. DRIVER TARRANT AND CONDUCTOR ROGERS. L.G.O.C. 20/10/15. E.S. 2.

5

Growth and unification: the London General Omnibus Company, 1920–30

David Lawrence

In the return to peacetime after the First World War, London once more experienced expansion and development as a mercantile and commercial capital. It still had substantial industrial areas close to the centre, served by thriving docks to the east, on and around the Isle of Dogs. Administrative activity for government, financial and commercial enterprises was predominantly manual in character, requiring large populations of office workers to flow in and out of the metropolis every day except Sunday. The advent of lifts and escalators enabled the development of the department store, replacing smaller shops in the West End and creating new travel patterns.

Central London's transport needs were met in the main by the activities of the Underground Group – an amalgamation of sub-surface and deep level railway lines with the London General Omnibus Company (LGOC) as the largest bus operator in the capital. The Group also included some tramway companies, power generating facilities and related businesses. This Combine made it possible to ever more fully co-ordinate transport networks. Key to this was the easing of interchange facilities, so that passengers found their journey from one transport to another both efficient and comfortable.

The Underground Group pursued a vigorous expansion programme, developing new railway lines into London's northern, western and southern areas. It built bus and tram stations alongside Underground stations, commissioning architects and graphic artists to provide exemplary design for buildings, signs and the publicity – posters, pocket maps, leaflets – which would encourage and improve travel. This growth was to provide better services, and to compete commercially with other transport operators such as the independents described in Chapter 6. Bus routes in central London, and into London's suburbs and the countryside of its home counties were augmented or added to the system by acquisition of other companies and inauguration of routes, throughout the 1920s.

Design of new Underground stations was paralleled by innovation in bus technology. The LGOC had been planning a new standard vehicle during the First World War, using American engineering expertise with its in-house team. The resulting bus, the K type, was launched in 1919. The S type followed in 1920, larger again than preceding models. Close relations between the LGOC and the AEC, backed by the finances of the Underground Group, promoted bus

FLEXIBILITY WOULD ENSURE SUPREMACY OF THE MOTOR BUS THROUGHOUT LONDON'S CENTRAL AND COUNTRY AREAS

development which combined design with mechanical innovation. The NS type of 1923 offered a lower access platform and, for the first time in London, the potential for a covered upper deck. In 1928 the NS type had solid tyres replaced by pneumatic rubber tyres. As the Underground continually refined its services within a totally designed environment, so the LGOC engineers continued to create new buses during the 1920s, of both double and single deck form. Most stayed in the capital; some were purchased for towns far from London, or overseas. This range of vehicles, at times leading the industry and at others following the competition, provided London with a transport legacy equal to the comfortable and efficient performance of its Underground railways.

Until July 1933, the LGOC buses ran alongside rail-bound trams and wire-bound trolleybuses provided by the London County Council, borough councils and Underground Group subsidiaries. Ultimately, the flexibility of the motor bus would ensure its supremacy for public transport throughout London's central and country areas.

George Shave, Chief Engineer to the LGOC in the period 1917-33, guided the design of all the buses discussed in this chapter. Mr Shave is at the Chiswick Works manufacturing and maintenance facility on 10 May 1923, to launch the latest vehicle development: the NS type bus.

2002/10043

The 46 seat K type bus, carrying 12 more passengers than
the B type, was a response to the relaxation of Metropolitan
Police controls over the size of buses which could be operated
on London streets. Introduced in August 1919, more than
1,000 vehicles were produced by the LGOC's manufacturing
subsidiary, the Associated Equipment Company, at its works in
Walthamstow, north east London. K types would work central
area routes, and join the fleets of operators with whom the
LGOC had business interests. Innovations in design evident
in the K type included rear wheel arches and straight sides,
which made it possible to have seats in pairs across the bus
body, rather than longitudinal benches. Wheels remained of
solid form. The bus's operator sat beside the engine, so that
the saloon could be extended forward for greater capacity.
In this picture K357 waits at the Warren Wood public house,
Buckhurst Hill, on a route 40A Sunday service to West
Norwood, circa 1922.

2002/10043

London's transport workers have a long-established tradition of charitable activities, often undertaken in their free time. Here, in August 1927, an outing to Epping Forest for under-privileged children has been organised by staff at Barking garage. Two men dressed as clowns are entertaining an audience watching from the upper deck and stairs of a K type bus. The bus driver, in his white dustcoat, is standing by the side of his vehicle.

1998/43659

In August 1921, the LGOC opened Chiswick Works in west London to provide centralised overhaul and construction facilities for its fleet of buses. Chief Engineer to the LGOC George Shave, arranged bus manufacture using the same assembly line practices as had been developed for motor car production. This is the facility bringing together the chassis frames and mechanical units onto which the bus bodies would later be fitted. On the right is the chassis of a K type bus that has just been overhauled. Engineers are reassembling the engine. Chiswick would become the base for the training school through which every grade of bus operating staff passed during their career. It was also the location for the store issuing uniforms to bus workers. Chiswick remained the primary London bus overhaul centre until the Aldenham maintenance complex in Hertfordshire opened fully in January 1956. Chiswick works closed completely in 1989.

2004/16639

The S type bus came into service in December 1920. This represented a further increase in size, accommodating 54 passengers. The S type was made heavier than the legal limit then in force, but its successful and safe operation led to a favourable change in Police regulations. In 1920, somewhere in west London, LGOC S type S1 passes an earlier model, B type B751, of the Metropolitan fleet.

1998/90045

To aid passengers and regularise bus operation, the Underground Group started experimenting with fixed stopping places, identified by a range of signs. This followed established tramway company practice. A limited system of fixed stops commenced in 1920. LGOC bus stops featured a sign marked with the red and blue bullseye symbol designed by calligrapher Edward Johnston. Here one is seen in Kingsway outside Holborn Underground station (below right). For Green Line coach stops, such as this one in Knightsbridge opposite Hyde Park (right), a variation of the LGOC sign was made, with a white symbol and lettering on a green ground. Bus services in country areas inspired designers to create less intrusive street furniture. At the Fox & Hounds public house, near Brasted, Kent, the stop flag is a simple silhouette made to emulate traditional inn signs.

2004/14466
2002/6505
2009/5823

The NS type bus was designed in 1923, with a new lower chassis and covered top. For safety reasons the Metropolitan Police would not approve a covered roof vehicle until 1925. Regulations such as these significantly hampered bus development. Pneumatic tyres were permitted in 1928, and an enclosed driver's cab was allowed in 1930. NS400 is shown with solid rubber tyres, in preserved condition.

2000/11406

Chiswick Works in west London was built to replace the LGOC many local garage repair facilities of variable standard, which had previously been used for vehicle maintenance. Buses were built, tested and overhauled here for some six decades, until privatisation removed the effective use of this single installation in the early 1980s. The site, which bordered the Underground's Acton railway repair workshops, has now been redeveloped as a business park.

1983/4/1150

IMPROVEMENT
No 6

L. G. O. C.
CENTRAL OVERHAUL
DEPOT

In order to standardize the work this Company has decided to establish a Central Overhaul Depot in place of carrying out the work at the various garages scattered throughout London. The result will be a quicker return to service of buses from overhaul, meaning more buses available for traffic. This New Depot is now being built

AT A COST OF OVER
£500,000

ELECTRIC RAILWAY HOUSE,
WESTMINSTER, LONDON, S.W.1.

GENERAL

The test track at Chiswick bus works in May 1923. Overhauled LGOC NS type bus chassis are being put through their paces, driven over the test track which included a 300-yard long man-made 'hill' with a gradient of 1 in 15.

2004/16625

Artist L B Black included an NS type bus in this 1926 poster promoting the hire of buses for use by private groups, rather than taking timetabled services. A trip to Surrey or Buckinghamshire was well within a day's travel, and for those without access to car, a convenient way to enjoy a good picnic.

1983/4/2075

The LGOC, working with independent and in-house architects, built many new garages as its network expanded and new vehicles joined the fleet. This is Barking Garage in Longbridge Road, Barking, east London, with an NS type in original form leaving for service in June 1926.

1998/89837

Designed by architect Charles Holden, the LGOC provided a motor bus station for visitors to the British Empire Exhibition of 1924 at Wembley, north west London. The station was notable for its brightly coloured shelters painted in an art deco style, and for the extensive signage to aid travellers. One particular sign is of interest – the disc and bar nameboard which follows the practice of signing stations established by the LGOC's parent company, the Underground Group. The Wembley facility could reportedly handle 200,000 visitors a day.

2004/11161

To provide more efficient interchange
between buses and other Underground
Group transport modes, bus stations
such as this one at Victoria were
developed through the 1920s and 1930s.

1998/80223

As the 1920s came to a close, bus operators in London and elsewhere adopted vehicles with two rear axles to support the additional weight of bodies built for larger passenger capacity. The LGOC had trialled the LS type from 1927; using the AEC's Renown chassis, it developed the LT type introduced in August 1929. Travelling south on Regent Street towards Piccadilly Circus, LT50 is of the early pattern with open external staircase.

1999/20448

Keenly aware of its heritage, the Underground Group commissioned this poster for the LGOC in 1929 to suggest its direct lineage to the first public buses in London. This poster by Richard T Cooper shows George Shillibeer's original 'omnibus', and an impression of the LGOC's newest vehicle, six-wheel LT type LT1.

2000/2233

At Merton LGOC bus garage in south London, LT type bus LT177 is in the process of having new exterior advertising panels applied. The complex livery used by the operator at this time – with different panels of colour and outlining, can be seen. The curious projection of the upper deck roof to serve as a sunshade is also evident.

1998/78902

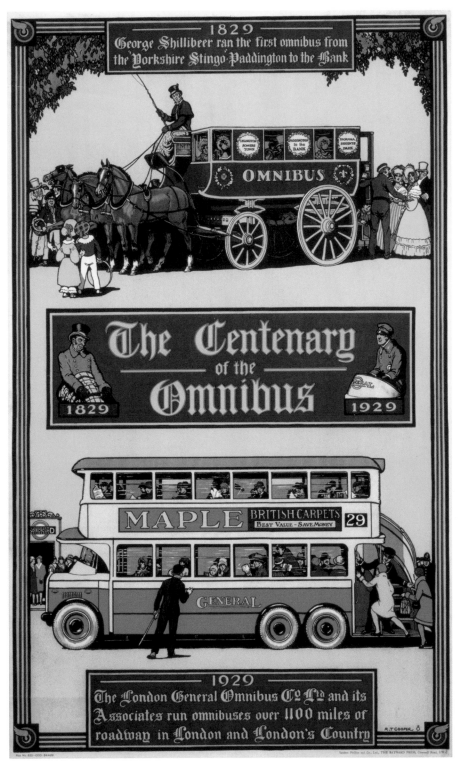

The 'pirate' buses 1922–33

Mike Sutcliffe MBE

After the First World War there was an acute shortage of motor buses. From 1919 new AEC K types, followed by the S type and NS type, brought more than 4,000 new buses into London General Omnibus Company (LGOC) service, but this still did not provide enough capacity for the growing demand. Whilst the 1920s saw a massive increase in bus and coach services throughout the country, with London initially leading developments, a shortage of buses continued to affect work and leisure in the capital.

On 5 August 1922, taxi driver Arthur Partridge put into service his brand new 48 seat double deck Leyland LB bus, working independently of the LGOC and with a virtual guarantee of custom. Men who returned from the First World War with the knowledge of how to drive and maintain heavy motor vehicles, would provide the manpower. Called the 'Chocolate Express' because of its livery colours, Partridge's bus was an instant success, and the first of over 250 independent 'pirate' operators that flourished across London from 1922 until 1933. Aware that others would soon follow, the LGOC aimed to crush this new competition. The public, however, warmed to Partridge's enterprising spirit and patronised his service. Newspapers criticised the unfair and bullying tactics of the LGOC and, following a deputation in the Chocolate Express bus to the Houses of Parliament, the LGOC abandoned their intimidation. There immediately followed a rapid expansion of new operators. Some – the true 'pirates' – were unscrupulous and, having chosen a route, might suddenly switch routes if a long queue of passengers for a different destination offered better business.

The majority of vehicle chassis used for independent buses were of designs developed from the War Office Subsidy Class A lorries of 1914–18. Robustly built but comparatively slow, these machines persisted until 1927. From 1925 there were a few new models, notably the introduction of the Leyland Lion and Dennis E single-deckers, used in small numbers. Inter-urban express services developed with fast and affordable machines like the very successful Gilford coaches. LGOC buses built by AEC, were of lighter construction but, there had been little development in body design. Significant design improvements emerged with G J Rackham's 'Tiger' and 'Titan', designed for Leyland in 1926. AEC had been through a difficult time, with reduced orders from London General, and a disastrous sales arrangement with Daimler. After AEC persuaded Rackham to join them as chief designer, he immediately produced an updated version of the 'Titan' and 'Tiger', instantly improving the company's fortunes. Thereafter, AEC and Leyland dominated the market in London, and in much of the British Isles.

OVER 250 'PIRATE' OPERATORS FLOURISHED ACROSS LONDON FROM 1922 UNTIL 1933

Towards the end of the 1920s, and following a number of serious accidents, there was an emphasis on safety for public service vehicles. Three-axle buses were coming into vogue, and were regarded as safer than the two-axle form, hence the name 'safety-six'. The extra seating capacity was considered an advantage for buses replacing tramcars. In London there were experiments with six-wheelers in the fleets of Pickup and London Public. The LGOC trialled its own six wheel bus, City built some too, and there were a few exotic examples such Westminster's 'Sunbeam Sikh', and City's three Leyland 'Titanics'. From late 1929 the LGOC adopted six-wheelers wholeheartedly, with the AEC Renown (the LT type) enabling a major fleet replacement programme to get underway.

The LGOC bought out as many operators as possible. Progress was slow until the London Traffic Act was passed in August 1924. A T Bennett, trading as 'Admiral', persuaded a number of independents to amalgamate, to protect their interests. They formed the London Public Omnibus Compnay in 1927. The high prices paid for buses made it an attractive option for the operators who joined London Public, only to find a year later that the business was taken over by the LGOC. The remaining 'pirates' continued until 1933-34 when they were compulsorily purchased, following the formation of the London Passenger Transport Board on 1 July 1933.

On an August Bank Holiday, outside St Martin-in-the-Field's, Trafalgar Square, this 34-seat B type won't make much of a dent in the long queue. The bus carries a post-war body and is in the livery of the Gearless Omnibus Company, a business taken over by the LGOC in 1913.

1998/45248

The 1920s and early 1930s was a colourful period for London's streets, with buses displaying a variety of liveries and imaginative fleet names. This Birch bodied AEC Regent of Red Line typifies the immaculate presentation of many of the 'pirate' buses, with its proud owners painting the tyres white every morning before it went out on service.

H C Casserley

UNDERGROUND
CHARING CROSS

In this crowded street scene in 1923, with LGOC buses barely able to cope with the number of potential customers at Charing Cross, we see a situation ripe for development by independent bus operators.
1998/44783

Arthur Partridge succeeded with his Chocolate Express business, increasing his fleet to six buses. A great character, he became Chairman of the Association of London Bus Proprietors Ltd, an organisation formed to protect the interests of the independent 'pirate' bus operators. This is Partridge's first bus, at Trafalgar Square when seven years old in 1929, clearly showing its white-walled tyres.

1998/31376

The 'Chocolate Express' (unnumbered bus in the centre of the photo right) in High Street, Kensington around 1922, is alone amidst a sea of LGOC buses. Bullying tactics used by the LGOC to get customers provoked a sympathetic response from the public who would deliberately wait for the 'Chocolate Bus'. The bus stop in the foreground is an early one; they were often sited opposite Underground stations.

1998/85535

Two London area managers from Leyland Motors, Crook and Mallender, left the company in January 1923 to form one of the first independents: the City Motor Omnibus Company. It grew to be one of the most respected of the 'pirates'. This was one of City's smart brown, yellow and cream Leyland LB5s, with Dodson body. For shoppers, a helpful revolving board below the route number says 'To & from Selfridges'.

Mike Sutcliffe collection

The Dennis 4 Ton was initially the most numerous of the first generation double deck 'pirate' buses. This one belonged to Cambrian, the biggest independent until its spectacular fall — by January 1926 the firm was bankrupt and absorbed by the LGOC.

W Noel Jackson

Redburns Motor Services were based in Ponders End and operated a large fleet of red and white vehicles. Their first 22 buses were built by Straker-Squire at Edmonton. Despite having an advanced design, the buses suffered with mechanical problems and most operators soon replaced them.

Mike Sutcliffe collection

Tilling-Stevens was a less popular manufacturer, but the TS3A, being petrol-electric, was easier to drive as it eliminated rough gear changes. However, it lacked power when climbing hills fully laden and often the passengers had to get off and follow on foot. Timpson's buses were painted silver.

Alan B Cross collection – J B Atkinson

Several operators catered to the increasing demand for bus and coach trips to the country and seaside resorts. Birch Bros operated this Tilling-Stevens TS3 charabanc, one of several registered in Ireland with the registration mark IT.

Mike Sutcliffe collection

Riding in an open coach or charabanc, like these LGOC Y types, was an exhilarating experience, though one had to be dressed for the weather. It would be a slow journey, averaging about 15 mph, even though the legal limit (usually ignored) was 12 mph.

1999/8091

Derby Day 1929 offered a great day out for Londoners and the top deck of the private hire K types made an ideal grandstand for watching the race.

1998/85894
1983/4/8886

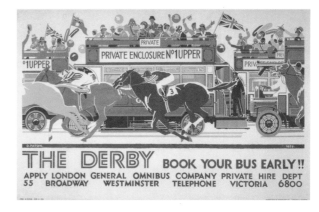

Here, a group representing the miners in the lead-up to the General Strike of May 1926, are taking the opportunity to use the top deck of a K type on its regular route through the city to promote a rally in Trafalgar Square. The strike was called by the Trade Union Congress in support of the miners, who were being threatened with longer hours at lower pay. The independent Cambrian company had recently been taken over by the LGOC and its livery was changed from green to red, but the Cambrian name on this bus remains.

Mike Sutcliffe collection

During the 1926 General Strike many independents, like the crowded Albert Ewer bus in this picture, continued to work alongside a reduced LGOC fleet. Routes were often improvised according to need, and destinations would be roughly chalked up, as seen here.

Mike Sutcliffe collection

A few independents used single-deckers on less busy routes. This 'Nil Desperandum' bus on route 202 is shown outside Surrey Docks Underground station in the early 1930s. The Leyland Lion was an advanced and successful vehicle, but restrictions imposed by the Metropolitan Police meant the vehicle was still without an enclosed cab, leaving the driver exposed to the elements.

Mike Sutcliffe collection

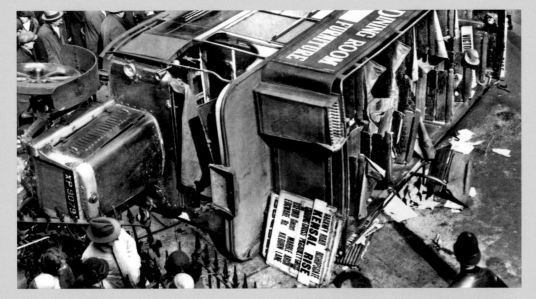

Accidents were not uncommon on the roads in the 1920s, but for motor buses in particular the consequences could be very serious. The *Evening News* of 10 April 1929 reported that this bus from the Gray fleet collided with a car and turned over, injuring all 50 passengers, including women and children. Bad publicity from accidents such as this could be damaging to small operators.

Mike Sutcliffe collection

Formed in 1927, the London Public Omnibus Company was one of the first of the London operators to employ 'Safety Six' omnibuses, which had six wheels. The buses, like this Guy FCX, provided a smooth and silent ride. It was also claimed the bus could lean at an angle of 50° without falling over.

Mike Sutcliffe collection

On 30 June 1928 the *Daily News and Westminster Gazette* announced the arrival of Charles Pickup's unique open top six-wheeled bus. Despite the innovative Guy FCX chassis and pneumatic tyres, Pickup continued to use open tops, possibly because his routes carried a lot of summer leisure traffic and he believed his passengers preferred this.

Mike Sutcliffe collection

As the trend towards six-wheeled buses continued, the LGOC responded to competition with their own version, the LS type, known as the 'London Six'. Unfortunately, with a high 68-seat capacity and small engine they were grossly under-powered for the task. They were not a success, so only 12 were built.

1998/30326

The City Motor Omnibus Company surprised everybody when they introduced three Leyland Titanics in 1933 with rather outdated Dodson 62 seat bodies with open stairs. They were, however, magnificent looking machines though the choice of model name for such large buses seems questionable.

H C Casserley

A rare model was the Daimler CF6, this example with Birch body being owned by Eagle. There were only two buses in the Eagle fleet at any one time, and, together with a Leyland Titan TD2, this CF6 was absorbed into the London Transport fleet as DST4 in November 1933.

Mike Sutcliffe collection

Overground was inaugurated in May 1926 to take over buses operated by Carlton and Dangerfield. The choice and design of the company name with upper case O and D is clearly intended to imply an association with the UndergrounD. Having built up a sizeable fleet of Dennis and Leyland vehicles, Overground was sold to the LGOC in June 1927. It was kept as a subsidiary and a large fleet of Dennis Lances, with LGOC designed ST-type bodies, was purchased. Here are three of them, around 1930, with D8 at the head of the queue.

Omnibus Society Archive – E G P Masterman

The last independents disappeared from London's streets in December 1934, and London Transport became sole provider of all bus services in the London area. A final dinner was held to wind up the Association of London Omnibus Proprietors in February 1936, with entertainment provided by the Billy Cotton dance band. Arthur Partridge of Chocolate Express gave the final address and one of his buses was pictured on the cover of the dinner programme. This marked the close of a very colourful era.

Mike Sutcliffe collection

By 1930 the LGOC was carrying 95% of London bus passengers and the end of the 'pirates' was in sight. Gordon Omnibus Co, was a typical small operator with a mixed fleet of seven buses. It was compulsorily purchased by the LPTB in December 1933 and vehicles like the Maudslay, pictured here in an anonymous London Transport yard, were consigned to private hire duties.

Mike Sutcliffe collection

Country Bus and Green Line

Laurie Akehurst

The origins of the London Transport Country Area stem from the desire of the London General Omnibus Company (LGOC) to provide services within a 25 mile radius from Central London. Operating agents were employed to run these routes, with the organisation becoming consolidated as London General Country Services in 1932. Green Line Coaches, which provided an express service from peripheral towns to and across London, was established in 1930. With the formation of the London Passenger Transport Board (LPTB) in July 1933 these services became the responsibility of the Country Buses and Coaches operating department.

Under London Transport the services were reorganised and new, purpose designed buses and coaches replaced much of the existing fleet. The Second World War saw a vast expansion of the aircraft industry, an outward movement of population and large numbers of military personnel being located in the Country Bus area. As a result, travel increased to nearly 260 million journeys per annum after the war, representing a staggering 90 per cent advance over pre-war levels.

The Green Line network – which had been withdrawn during the war – was reinstated in 1946, and London Transport drew up plans to replace existing vehicles and allow for future expansion. The Town and Country Planning Act of 1947 proposed the building of a number of new towns of which Crawley, Harlow, Hatfield, Hemel Hempstead, Stevenage and Welwyn Garden City were located in the Country Bus area. By 1954 the pre-war fleet had been replaced with new buses which gave a great degree of standardisation. Demands for bus travel peaked in the mid-1950s, but in a period of post-war affluence, constantly rising car ownership levels and the spread of television, leisure travel by bus was in serious decline. The six week bus strike of 1958 did further damage, causing considerable passenger losses. Country Bus and Green Line operations experienced a spiral of passenger decline and corresponding service cuts during the 1960s, with the situation being exacerbated by worsening staff shortages. By the middle of the decade, the introduction of high capacity one-man operated vehicles was seen as the way forward. Negotiations on this proposal with the trade union, however, were both complex and protracted. Finally in 1968 the new buses were introduced and a start was also made to convert Green Line coaches to one-man operation.

TRAVEL IN THE COUNTRY BUS AREA INCREASED BY 90 PER CENT AFTER WORLD WAR TWO

In 1970 the Greater London Council assumed control of London Transport, with the Country Buses and Coaches department being reconstituted as London Country Bus Services Ltd, a subsidiary of the National Bus Company. The new operator inherited an ageing fleet of vehicles which it replaced with new, but often less reliable models, and it was dogged with continuing staff shortages and falling passenger numbers. Loss-making services were funded by local authorities, with the routes being tailored to local needs. Green Line coach operations were completely revamped with an expansion of services to new destinations. As a prelude to privatisation, London Country was split into four operating companies in 1986. The deregulation of the bus industry and private ownership meant that many more changes were to come, but the name Green Line continues as a marketing entity to this day.

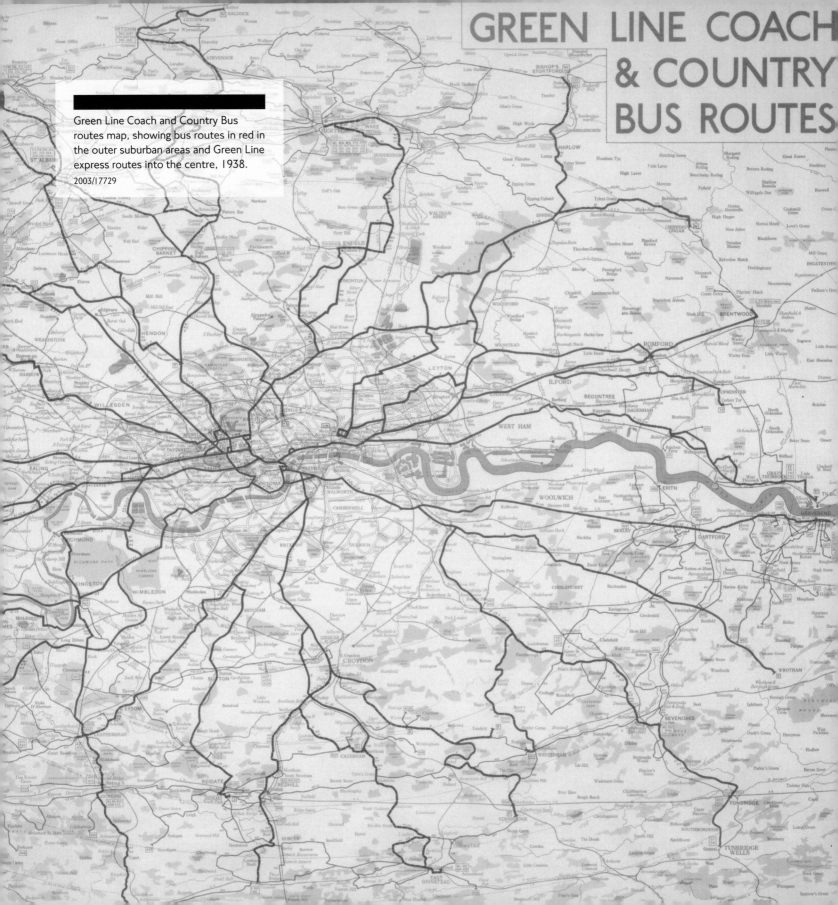

GREEN LINE COACH & COUNTRY BUS ROUTES

Green Line Coach and Country Bus routes map, showing bus routes in red in the outer suburban areas and Green Line express routes into the centre, 1938.

2003/17729

The LGOC commenced operations in Watford, Hertfordshire, in 1920, but disputes over varying rates of pay caused industrial unrest. In 1921, the LGOC – which provided the buses and garages – approached the National Omnibus & Transport Co Ltd, to operate services in its northern area. The origin of National, with operations based on Bedford, Chelmsford, Stroud and Yeovil, went back to Thomas Clarkson's steam bus empire. Bus B 5099 is a single deck B type seating 26 passengers and is here operating from Watford to Harrow on route N16, which established a new link running via Rickmansworth and Northwood.

Ken Glazier collection

In 1922 the LGOC entered into an agreement with the Reigate-based East Surrey Traction Company to operate services within a defined area. This AEC S type with a Short Brothers body dating from 1922 (registration number PC9318), was number 95 in the East Surrey fleet. Route S24 linked Reigate with Sevenoaks. The crew stand by their vehicle, the conductor wearing a Bell Punch machine and the driver being well wrapped up as there is no windscreen. The bus advertises East Surrey's char-a-banc excursions to Brighton for five shillings, and to Eastbourne for seven shillings and six pence.

Alan B Cross – G. Robbins collection

Due to expansion of services an additional garage was opened at Hatfield, Hertfordshire, in 1922. We see a number of staff assembled for the photograph, dressed in their summer uniforms with two sporting bow ties! The 'guv'nor' has been granted the courtesy of a chair. The bus carries boards for route N10 which ran between St. Albans and Hertford, providing a link across an area previously only served by infrequent trains. Bus NS 1100, was supplied by the LGOC and never received a covered top body, being taken out of stock in January 1936.

Alan B Cross – G Robbins collection

Large operators took a dim view of independents running within their established areas. Sevenoaks Motor Service started a service between Sevenoaks and Shoreham Village, so East Surrey introduced competing route 401E over the same roads in April 1930. Some passengers chose to remain loyal to the independent, but the competition proved too much for the small concern, and it sold out to East Surrey in November 1930. This Commer Invader with an 18-seat Weymann body was ideal for rural routes running through narrow lanes, where passengers were sparse. Vehicles with 20 seats or less could be worked by just one man.

J F Higham collection

From 1 March 1932 East Surrey and National were unified as London General Country Services (LGCS). NS 1072 stands in Kingsbury Square, Aylesbury on route 301. Originally fitted with solid tyres the bus now has pneumatic tyres, an improvement introduced in the late 1920s. To meet a requirement of the London Traffic Act, 1924, the Metropolitan Police directed that any routes entering its area from the north should be numbered from 301 upwards, and those entering from the south be numbered from 401 upwards. This was the origin of London Transport's Country Bus route numbering arrangements.

Alan B Cross – W. Noel Jackson collection

In the late 1920s a number of coach operators established express services into central London which offered an attractive alternative to train travel, and abstracted longer distance passengers from LGOC bus services. One such was Premier Line which ran from Windsor and Beaconsfield via Slough to Aldwych. This smartly turned out Leyland Tiger coach in red and cream livery is on the Windsor route. The LPTB had powers to compulsorily acquire many such operators. Premier Line was taken over in December 1933, with this coach eventually being passed from London Transport to Thames Valley Traction Company.

J F Higham collection

As Green Line services expanded, a further batch of AEC Regals with a front entrance was placed into service; here one is seen in Piccadilly Circus heading for Chelsham on route J in 1932. The scene is completed by LGOC buses in profusion and limousine style motorcars. Southern Railway trains from the area served by the coach would have taken passengers to Victoria or London Bridge termini, but the great advantage of Green Line was that it took passengers into the very heart of the West End.

1998/44907

Green Line coach services commenced in 1930, in response to many independent operators which had established routes. T 141, an AEC Regal with 27-seat bodywork by Hall Lewis (later to become Park Royal Vehicles), is seen on Victoria Embankment running to Brentwood. Green Line offered deeper, more comfortable seats and the curtains clearly imply a touch of luxury. The actions of careless smokers resulted in the removal of curtains at an early stage, whilst passengers continued to enjoy the convenience of luggage racks, a mirror and a clock. The coach conductor is equipped with an ancient pistol punch, rather than a Bell Punch ticket machine.

1999/20433

London Transport had powers to compulsorily acquire independent concerns running services within its 'Special Area'. One of many to be taken over was Flower & Etches which used the fleetname 'City'. The company dated from 1923, and when acquired in March 1934 was running two routes from St. Albans to Welwyn Garden City and Codicote. This GMC 20-seater of 1929 (UR4328) in blue and yellow livery, is seen setting down passengers in St. Peter's Street, St. Albans outside Woolworth's 3d and 6d Stores. It saw little work with London Transport, being withdrawn later in 1934.

J F Higham collection

The first new buses delivered to the Country area comprised a batch of 12 AEC Regals with 48-seat low-height bodies built by Weymann. They were urgently needed to replace ancient open toppers on route 410 from Bromley to Reigate, which passed under a low bridge in Oxted. Country Bus & Coach operating manager A H Hawkins, favoured a front entrance layout with a sliding door. The distinctive London Transport underlined fleetname was not adopted until May 1934 and buses continued to be fitted with the General transfer. Most of the class were allocated to Godstone Garage and, not surprisingly, became known as 'Godstone STLs'.

1998/87720

Many one-man operated buses of a variety of types were inherited from the independent companies. To replace them on Country Area services, an order was made for 74 Leyland Cubs with 20-seat bodies by Short Brothers. In this view two gentlemen smoking pipes are about to board C 3 outside Longfield Station (then known as Fawkham Station) while working on route 490 between Longfield Hill and Gravesend. The bus is in the two-tone green Country area livery of the mid-1930s. One-man drivers were paid an extra five shillings per week to collect fares and issue tickets.

Topfoto

To provide the front entrance buses preferred by the Country area's operating manager, a batch of 85 specially designed STLs, fitted with 48-seat bodies, were built by London Transport at Chiswick Works and delivered in 1935. Due to the demands for travel caused by the Second World War their seating capacity was subsequently increased to 52. STL 1007 is working on route 401 which ran between Sevenoaks and Gravesend via Farningham and Dartford. The Central Area practice of buses carrying running numbers was extended to the Country area in 1934.

M Gaywood

The popularity of motor coach services caused congestion at terminal points such as Charing Cross and Oxford Circus. Under powers in the Road Traffic Act, 1930, the newly established traffic commissioner sought to impose stringent restrictions on the services. This culminated in a commission of inquiry being established under Lord Amulree. The findings resulted in a revised Green Line network from October 1933 with most services based on Eccleston Bridge, Victoria, and cross London running much extended. In this August 1937 view holiday crowds board brand new T 452 which is running from Leatherhead to Baldock on route K1.

1998/85289

With increasing conscription into the armed services women conductors, were employed in the Country Area from July 1940. By 1942 women accounted for 83 per cent of conductors and 57 per cent of garage engineering general hands. In this posed view a newly recruited female conductor discusses the intricacies of the vehicle running card with her driver. It was envisaged that women would step down after the war but, in a rather different post-war world, London Transport experienced great difficulty in recruiting and retaining male staff. Women were destined to remain as conductors until the end of crew operation.

Fox Photos

A revised Green Line network was introduced in December 1940, with double deck buses replacing the single deck coaches on some routes. STL 1497 was one of a further order of 50 front entrance buses delivered in the second part of 1936. This batch had Weymann built bodies featuring many differences from the earlier Chiswick-bodied examples. STL 1497 is in simplified war-time Lincoln green and white livery, and has been fitted with anti-blast netting on some of the non-opening windows. It is seen in Romford prior to working a journey on the busy route 55 to Aldgate.

The Omnibus Society

The extra demand for travel in the Country Area since the outbreak of the war meant that buses had to be transferred from the Central Area to meet the increased demand. Red STL 2410, dating from 1938 and allocated to Amersham Garage, waits outside the pleasing frontage of Windsor Garage before working to Berkhamsted on lengthy route 353. The bus is fitted with reduced area destination blinds which were introduced in 1942 to save linen and paper. A number of buses transferred from the Central area were eventually repainted into green livery but this bus was not so treated.

The Omnibus Society

By the end of the war, government-imposed restrictions on bus building meant that London Transport was forced to implement a policy of make do and mend. Demand for travel was high and some relief came in 1946 with the purchase of 20 AEC Regent Mark II chassis fitted with standard Weymann bodies. The vehicles were classified 18STL20, numbered STL 2682-2701, and were allocated to Watford High Street Garage. STL 2695, in the war-time Lincoln green and white livery, is seen with a good load of passengers heading for Rickmansworth. Some people evidently found it more convenient to cycle.

Alan B Cross

Withdrawn in September 1942 as a wartime economy measure, the Green Line coach network was reintroduced between February and June 1946 as resources became available. This was seen as a major step in restoring peace-time conditions. The new network was slimmed down by almost a quarter compared with pre-war levels, requiring 248 coaches. In a rare colour view Q 208 sets down passengers at Hertford Bus Station having just completed the 59 mile journey from Guildford. Q 208 was one of a batch of 50 vehicles introduced in 1936–37, representing the Green Line version of the Q type, designated 6Q6.

Alan B Cross

In 1942 buses which served certain armament manufacturing establishments were painted in grey livery. This posed view shows a military policewoman in front of Q 40: note the heavily masked headlights which would not have been effective during the black-out. The bus was one of three in grey allocated to Reigate Garage to work on route 440 to the Monotype Factory at Salfords. The grey livery was discontinued late in 1944. The Q type was a revolutionary design with a full front and off-side mounted engine. Classified 4Q4, the Country Bus version, dated from 1935 and consisted of 102 vehicles.

Getty Images

To replace its single deck fleet London Transport developed the RF type which comprised an AEC Regal IV chassis with an engine similar to that of the RT but side-mounted and a body by Metropolitan-Cammell. The Green Line version consisted of 263 coaches, with the first one entering service to much publicity in October 1951. Vehicles were finished in Lincoln green livery with a light green relief around the windows, and seated 39 passengers with all but one seat facing forwards. RF75 is seen at All Souls Church, Langham Place, central London on route 715 running from Hertford to Guildford.

1998/86984

Low railway bridges sometimes prevented conventional double-deckers passing beneath, requiring buses with special low-height bodies. The British Transport Commission offered London Transport 20 buses originally intended for Midland General but rendered surplus. Weymann bodies, which had an off-side sunken gangway on the upper deck with seats in rows of four arranged on the near-side, were fitted to AEC Regent Mark III chassis. A further batch of 56 buses of this RLH type was subsequently placed in service. RLH 36 is seen passing under the low railway bridge in Bluehouse Lane, Oxted while working between Reigate and Bromley on route 410.

Alan B Cross

The Country Area received RT type vehicles from July 1948, enabling the ST type and subsequently STL type, to be withdrawn. RT 974 was new to Hertford Garage in October 1948, for routes 310 (Hertford – Enfield) and 310A (Rye House – Enfield) and is at Enfield Town terminus. The livery is Lincoln green with a cream centre band and upper deck window surrounds, the latter being subsequently discontinued. The bodies were fitted with a roof route number box which was another feature discontinued with later deliveries. The bus has the reduced area destination blinds which had been introduced during the war.

The Omnibus Society

London Transport could not justify the development of a special design for the replacement of its small one-man operated single deck fleet, and approached Guy Motors for a vehicle based on their Otter and Vixen models. Attractive 26 seat bodies finished in Lincoln green were ordered from Eastern Coach Works. The vehicles were known as 'Guy Specials', thus giving the classification GS. During 1953-54, 84 buses were commissioned, for use mostly on services where the lanes were narrow and passengers were sparse. GS 77 is in Windsor High Street running on route 445, the short link with Datchet Common.

Alan B Cross

The Country Bus version of the RF was introduced from March 1953 and together with the GS type enabled the withdrawal of all pre-war single-deckers by 1954. The RF buses were finished in Lincoln green with cream window surrounds and seated 41 passengers. Following successful experiments, during 1956-59 they were equipped for one-man operation, which involved the loss of two seats. This saved the cost of conductors on rural services where passenger numbers had declined. RF 564, fitted with signage for one-man operation, awaits further custom at St. Mary's Square, Hitchin in the early 1960s.

Alan B Cross

As far as Country Buses were concerned the decline in bus travel dating from the mid-1950s was partially offset by the growth of the New Towns, which continued to expand throughout the 1960s and beyond. Local routes were established to meet the needs of workers, shoppers and school children. London Transport built new garages in Hatfield and Stevenage in 1959 and in Harlow in 1963 to cater for increases in the numbers of buses needed to serve the growing communities. In this view RT 4043 is seen in Hodings Road, Harlow heading for Little Parndon on route 805.

Alan B Cross

Following the evaluation of a prototype Routemaster Green Line coach it was decided to use such vehicles on busier routes, bringing economies by reducing service frequencies and duplication. Sixty-eight vehicles designated RMC (Routemaster Coach) entered service between August 1962 and January 1963. They were finished to full Green Line standards with deeper and more generously spaced seats, luggage racks and platform doors, and proved very popular with the passengers who welcomed the sightseeing opportunities offered by the upper deck. RMC 1499 passes St. Peter's Church, Bushey Heath while running on route 719 from Victoria to Hemel Hempstead.

1998/85293

Green Line routes 721 and 722 from Aldgate to Brentwood and Upminster commenced operation using austerity-standard Daimler vehicles in 1946. These were replaced in 1950 by a batch of 36 RTs in Green Line livery, joined by a further 21 in 1954 on the 723 group of routes from Aldgate to Grays and Tilbury. In 1965 the RTs were replaced by 43 RCL vehicles, the lengthened version of the RMC. Here driver Kerrigan and conductor Eavis of Romford, London Road Garage, stand with RT 3230 early in 1965 on the cobblestones at Aldgate Bus and Coach Station before departing for Brentwood. Aldgate was an important transport hub at the edge of London's financial and mercantile district.

Remember When

In the mid-1960s the future RF Green Line fleet was reviewed. It was decided to radically improve both their exteriors and interiors and London Transport engaged the services of design consultant Misha Black from Design Research Unit. Black's revision of the 175 coaches was striking, featuring a two-tone green livery with a broad waist-band, twin headlamps, repositioned turn indicators, and other detail differences. The refurbished interiors were fitted with fluorescent lighting and finished in the style of the Routemaster coaches. RF 94 stands at Crawley Bus Station bound for Chesham on route 710, together with RF and RT Country Area buses.

Alan B Cross

During the mid-1960s a new generation of rear-engine, front entrance vehicles were evaluated. Designated the XF class, eight Daimler Fleetlines with Park Royal bodies, were purchased for use in the Country Area. They entered service in September 1965 working from East Grinstead Garage, principally on route 424 (East Grinstead – Reigate) and were initially operated with both a driver and conductor. Regulations at the time did not allow double deck operation by just the driver, so an experiment in one man operation was devised whereby the upper deck was locked out of use and passengers were confined to the lower deck at slack times when only a driver was used. The experiment did not prove to be a success. This view shows XF 8 departing from Reigate Station for East Grinstead.

Lyndon Rowe

To work on some of the busier routes, 100 RMLs were delivered to the Country Area in 1965-66. They seated 72 passengers compared to the RT's 56, which enabled frequency reductions and consequent savings in the numbers of both buses and crews required. RML 2425 is working on route 346C, one of a number of services run solely for school children. The bus advertises Green Rover tickets: these has been introduced in 1956 and offered unlimited travel on most Country Bus routes, proving to be very popular with those seeking a day out in the country.

J G S Smith

London Transport's *Bus Reshaping Plan* of 1966 placed its faith in high capacity single-deckers of a new and untested design - the AEC Merlin. For busy town services, high capacity standee buses were introduced, offering a mere 25 seats, and standing space for 41 passengers. They were equipped with two Autoslot ticket machines operated by the passengers upon boarding. Both the buses and the ticket machines proved unreliable and unpopular with passengers, who perceived them as vastly inferior to the buses that they had displaced. MBS 271 is working on route 430 which ran between Redhill and Reigate.

2005/14764

By the mid-1970s service cuts and the use of unsuitable Leyland National vehicles meant that Green Line services had lost a considerable number of passengers. From 1977 the company took action and remodelled the route network using motorway running and also introduced new routes to London's Airports. Legislation of 1980 allowed Green Line to run out further to new destinations in some cases jointly with other bus companies. A batch of 150 new AEC Reliance coaches in a striking white and green livery was leased. Duple bodied RB80 is seen on route 705 taking on passengers in Westerham.

Barry Le Jeune

When London Country Bus Services Ltd. took control of the London Transport Country Area in 1970, approximately 70 per cent of the fleet dated from the 1950s and was in need of replacement. Most routes were running at a loss and a policy of 100 per cent one-person operation was to be implemented. From 1972 Leyland Nationals in various sub-types were purchased until, over a seven year period, the company had the dubious distinction of being the largest operator of the type in the UK with some 543 buses in ownership. In this view SNB331 is at Crawley Bus Station on route 434 heading for Crawley Down.

Barry Le Jeune

8

The London bus in
popular
culture
1829–2014

Simon Murphy

The French division of The Who's record company chose this classic 'London Transport double decker in Piccadilly Circus' type image for the picture sleeve of *Magic Bus* in 1968, while the bus on the cover of the UK LP we have had more in common with the Merry Pranksters' psychedelic school bus.

www.popsike.com

PEOPLE ALL OVER THE WORLD
KNOW THAT LONDON BUSES ARE RED.

When route tendering brought multi-coloured buses to our streets in the 1980s, tourists were confused and Londoners unsettled, until Transport for London decided to restore their redness. The man on the Clapham omnibus breathed a sigh of relief.

Buses were not always red, but their association with London goes back a long way. Horse buses became a city fixture soon after Shillibeer's first services in 1829, but it was the Great Exhibition of 1851 in Hyde Park that brought images of bus travel and traffic to a wider public. Bus-themed cartoons were a staple of the new illustrated magazines then appearing; postcards and the popular songs of the music hall completed the picture later.

The coming of the motor bus gave cartoonists and commentators the opportunity to question or satirise modernity and progress. When the London General Omnibus Company (LGOC) upgraded their horse buses to red motor buses before the First World War, they started a process that would make the big red bus completely synonymous with London by the outbreak of the Second World War, 25 years later.

On film the convention of using a passing bus to signify London, was established early, in D W Griffith's *Broken Blossoms* of 1919. It has been employed in countless films and television shows ever since. This bright, everyday icon is cheap, easy to locate and above all mobile, allowing any city or studio set to be instantly understood as London.

Buses became an almost universal symbol of the metropolis, but in the 1960s the whole situation moved up another gear. Starting with *Summer Holiday* in 1963, starring Cliff Richard and chums travelling across Europe in a converted RT type, it mushroomed from there. Suddenly buses were everywhere: on tv and in films, on vinyl record covers, and overflowing from toy shops, merging with the camp psychedelic nostalgia swirl of Swinging London.

As the 1960s lurched into the 1970s, Saturday morning television was brightened up by a pre-teen gang who used an old bus as their clubhouse – they were the *Double Deckers*. As real-world bus services continued their steep decline, positive sightings of buses became less frequent. The tv comedy *On The Buses* featured a scheming, lazy bus driver and his sleazy conductor, embroiled in a series of tawdry adventures and slapstick scenes. Widely assumed to portray London, it was actually based in a fictional Essex town and shot partly in Eastern National's Wood Green depot.

The popular profile of the bus continued to shrink in the 1980s and 1990s. Duke Baysee, the singing conductor on route 38, got to number 30 in the UK charts in 1995, but he was not destined for stardom. The Spice Girls had a bus in their 1997 feature film *Spiceworld*, but it was from Birmingham. In the media your best chance of seeing a London bus would be one handcuffed to a disability rights campaigner. Harry Potter's 'Knight Bus' raised the stakes once more in 2004, and at the end of 2005, the world mourned the end of regular Routemaster services in London. A red double-decker featured heavily in the handover to London at the end of the 2008 Olympics in Beijing, alongside superstar footballer David Beckham and Mayor of London Boris Johnson.

2014 has been Transport for London's Year of the Bus, including the restoration of a B type from 1913, numerous garage open days and events, a parade of over 50 vintage vehicles down Regent Street, and – least likely of all – a special Routemaster-themed Fender 'Stratocaster' guitar. The man on the Clapham omnibus would be proud.

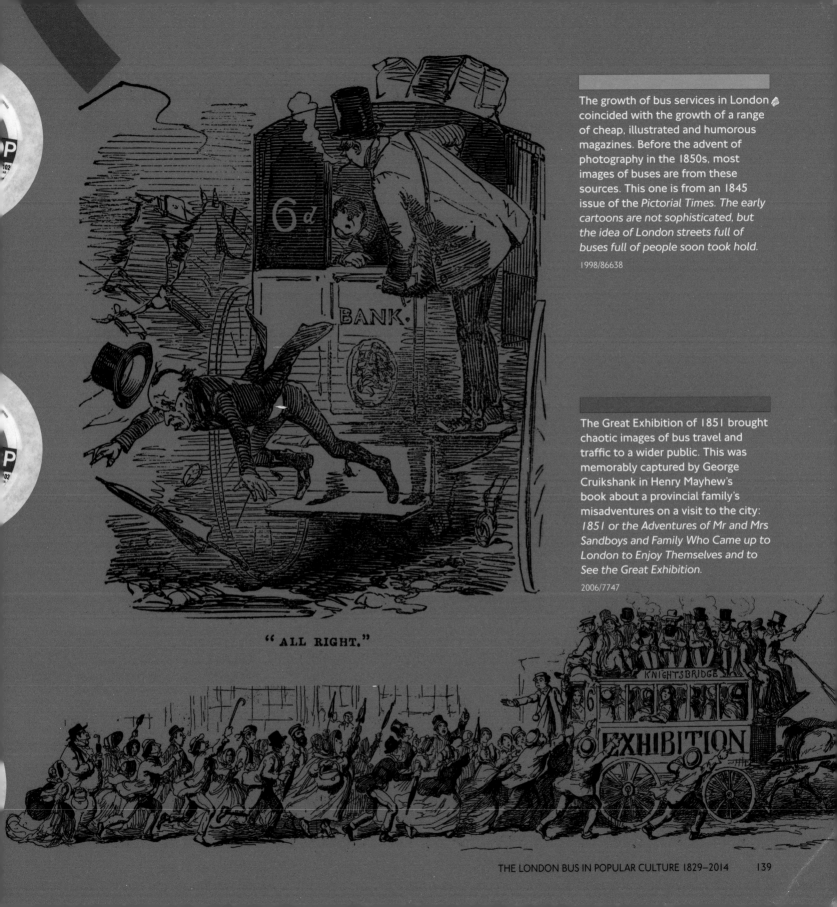

The growth of bus services in London coincided with the growth of a range of cheap, illustrated and humorous magazines. Before the advent of photography in the 1850s, most images of buses are from these sources. This one is from an 1845 issue of the *Pictorial Times*. *The early cartoons are not sophisticated, but the idea of London streets full of buses full of people soon took hold.*

1998/86638

The Great Exhibition of 1851 brought chaotic images of bus travel and traffic to a wider public. This was memorably captured by George Cruikshank in Henry Mayhew's book about a provincial family's misadventures on a visit to the city: *1851 or the Adventures of Mr and Mrs Sandboys and Family Who Came up to London to Enjoy Themselves and to See the Great Exhibition.*

2006/7747

"ALL RIGHT."

THE RIVAL OMNIBUSES.
STOP, SIR! LADIES FIRST.

Registered.

Horse bus travel proved a fertile subject for the music hall, with several songs featuring romance between drivers and female passengers. Ditties such as *Riding on the top of an omnibus* were something of a speciality of singer Arthur Lloyd in the 1860s.

Roger Torode collection

The competition between unregulated horse buses during the Great Exhibition and afterwards became a popular image of Victorian London. This is an early example of a comedy souvenir photographic print.

2005/13940

THE MOTOR 'BUS.

Fussy Old Gent. "STOP! STOP! I WANT TO GET DOWN." *Driver.* "I CAN'T STOP THE BLOOMIN' THING!!"

THE CAREER OF THE "TERROR."
If you're in a hurry—walk.

Pictorial postcards were introduced to the UK in 1894 and were an immediate success. They were cheap, widely available and very fast, with as many as 10 deliveries a day in London. Topical satirical cards were especially popular. This example, posted in 1909, shows an early motor bus the 'Terror' running over a pedestrian. The subtitle is 'if you're in a hurry — walk'.

2009/9191

"I can't stop the bloomin' thing!" exclaims a worried driver in this early jibe at the motorised bus by the famous caricaturist Phil May. It was drawn for *Punch* in 1896, at least two years before the first motor bus services in London. What he shows of the vehicle is closer to one of Walter Hancock's steam carriages of the 1830s than any real bus.

2014/6306

STEREO

NANCY IN LONDON

6 B

Frank Sinatra'a daughter Nancy had a busy 1966. *These Boots Are Made for Walkin'* was a worldwide hit, and she recorded three albums. She poses slightly awkwardly on the front of a groovy Routemaster for the cover of the third.

Simon Murphy collection

"Doing her Bit"

FARES PLEASE.

Another postcard from around 1916, by Flora White, best known as an illustrator of J M Barrie's Peter Pan books. The cutesy image of a child-like female bus conductor 'doing her bit' seems patronising to modern eyes, but such portrayals were popular and widespread.

2013/8058

A bus shelter full of people in Holloway Road, north London, 1939. *Lightning Conductor*, starring the popular British comedian Gordon Harker as a busman, is showing at the Marlborough cinema behind them.

1998/26614

Although only 17 episodes of *Here Come The Double Deckers* were produced, between 1970 and 1972, the series was repeated well into the mid-1970s, spawning a novel, a colouring book, a soundtrack LP and this annual. Brinsley Forde, who played Spring, later sang with the British reggae band Aswad.

Simon Murphy collection

THE DOUBLE DECKERS

annual 1972

THE RIOTOUS
ADVENTURES OF
TV's HAPPIEST GANG

Authorised edition based on
the popular Television Series

Used buses were plentiful in the 1960s and 70s, and were converted to everything from this trendy mobile boutique selling paper dresses for 19 shillings each, to a slightly incongruous Camden estate agent. This tradition has been revived in recent years, with converted Routemasters selling anything from frozen yoghurt and cocktails to pizzas and M&Ms confectionery.

Harry Dempster

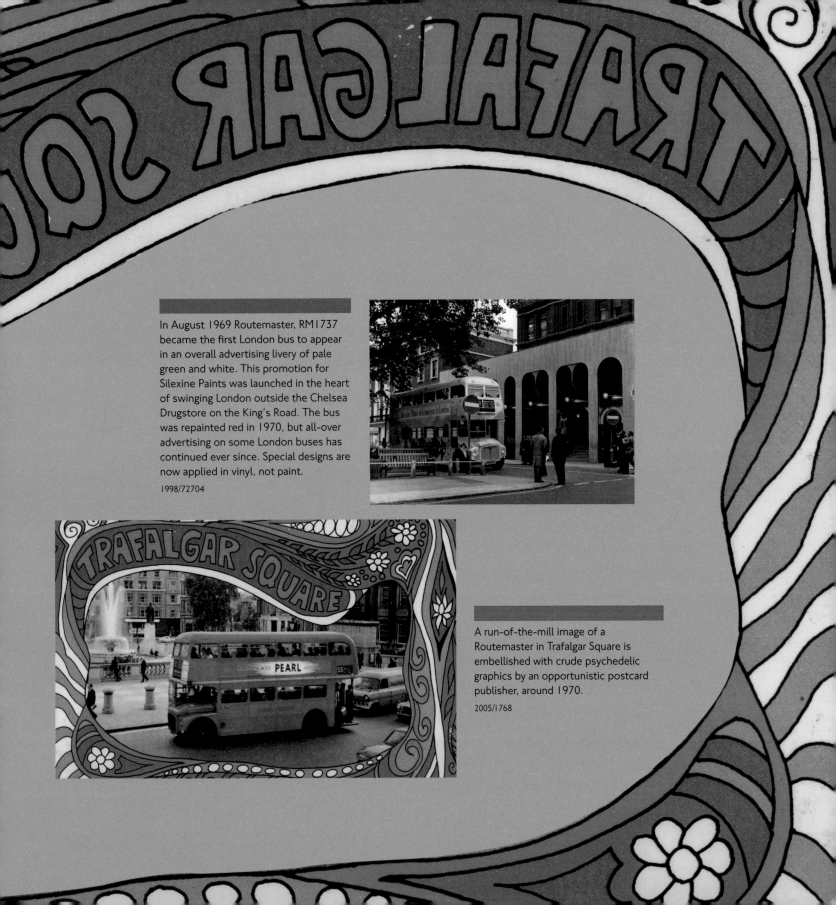

In August 1969 Routemaster, RM1737 became the first London bus to appear in an overall advertising livery of pale green and white. This promotion for Silexine Paints was launched in the heart of swinging London outside the Chelsea Drugstore on the King's Road. The bus was repainted red in 1970, but all-over advertising on some London buses has continued ever since. Special designs are now applied in vinyl, not paint.

1998/72704

A run-of-the-mill image of a Routemaster in Trafalgar Square is embellished with crude psychedelic graphics by an opportunistic postcard publisher, around 1970.

2005/1768

Bus Stop Records was formed in 1972 by pop hitmakers Mitch Murray and Peter Callender as an outlet for their songs. Their biggest hit was *Billy Don't Be A Hero*, a number one for Paper Lace in 1974.

1998/3553

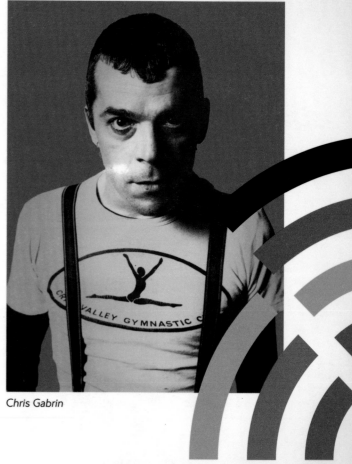

Chris Gabrin

'The Busman's Prayer' had been circulating in the bus workforce in various versions for many years. The most popular version known today is Ian Dury's rendition, performed with his band the Blockheads. Dury may have learned the poem from his father, a bus driver, remembered in the song *My Old Man*.

Our father, who art in Hendon.

Harrow Road be thy name.

Thy Kingston come thy Wimbledon, in

Erith as it is in Hendon.

Give us this day our Berkhamstead and

forgive us our Westminsters, as we forgive

those who Westminster against us

For thine is the Kingston, the Purley and

the Crawley. For Iver and Iver, Crouch End.

Released in 1979, and reaching number 23 in the charts, *Boogie Bus* was one of the first generation of dance compilation albums programmed and segued by professional DJs. The design mimics the front of a red bus, but without huge attention to detail. The 'route number' gives the number of tracks.

Simon Murphy collection

Backpackers and tourists decorated jackets and bags with sew-on patches like this one in the 1970s. While other cities might be represented by a coat of arms or the silhouette of an iconic building, this 'London' patch deftly illustrates the equation of the city and its big red bus, in this case a crudely executed Routemaster.

David Lawrence collection

Production design researchers visited the London Transport Museum collections in 2003, while investigating buses that could be used as the basis for the purple triple deck Knight Bus first seen in the film *Harry Potter and the Prisoner of Azkaban* the following year. The final bus is an amalgamation of two RT type buses.

Inspired Adornations

London Transport used a strangely deadpan reference to the Wham! hit *Wake Me Up Before You Go-Go* to promote one day bus passes in 1986.

1987/54/1

Two young film producers, Jane Saunders and Lucy Main, launched the 'Farewell Routemaster' film challenge on 2 December 2005, 'to preserve, in a unique way, the cultural heritage of this beautiful bus and to provide filmmakers with an opportunity to say a proper good-bye to the bus that has been the definitive face of London in documentaries and fiction films for decades'.

The winning film can be seen here: www.edhartwell.co.uk/buskong.html

2008/963

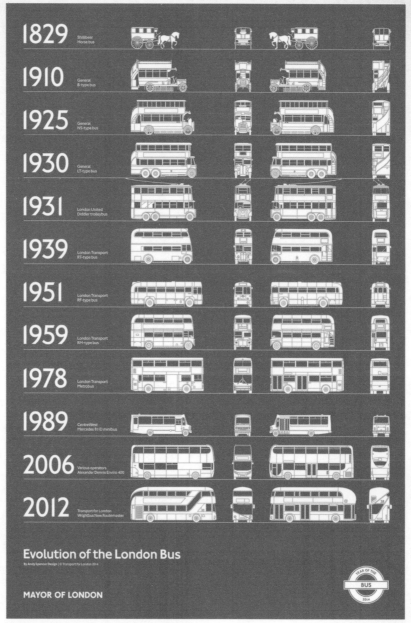

A popular poster, commissioned for TfL's Year Of The Bus 2014, summarises the evolution of London's signature vehicle.

LTM Design

The Museum's newly restored B type at Stockwell garage in the build up to the biggest single event of the Year of the Bus - the Cavalcade, in June 2014. Vehicles spanning the last 185 years lined up in chronological order on Regent Street between Piccadilly and Oxford Circus.

Tim Shields

One of the more unusual events for the Year of the Bus was the launch of a limited edition guitar, styled like a 1950s bus, complete with 'moquette' scratchplate! The Routemaster-themed Fender Stratocaster is the product of a happy coincidence that nobody seems to have noticed before; the unveiling of the first prototype of the iconic Routemaster bus in London and the launch of the ultra-modern Stratocaster guitar by Leo Fender in Bakersfield, California were just a few months apart, in 1954. Twenty five 'Routecasters' were produced to mark this joint anniversary, which also includes Strat-themed New Routemaster buses on TfL's 'musical heritage' route 24.

TfL Press Office

9

Creating London Transport – the 1930s

Oliver Green

By the early 1930s the cheap and convenient bus had become London's most popular form of public transport. Passenger journeys by road and rail in Greater London had increased by 30 per cent during the 1920s, but this overall travel figure hid striking variations between modes. Underground and local railway traffic grew steadily, use of the trams remained constant but bus travel boomed. The total number of bus journeys made had more than doubled in a decade.

The LGOC, working with its main bus supplier AEC, continued to make rapid progress in vehicle development and engineering at Chiswick. New buses were increasingly reliable, easier to maintain and most importantly, attractive and comfortable for passengers. The LT, ST and T type were all developed in 1929 in a major fleet replacement programme, with large orders for engines and chassis built by AEC at its new Southall plant in west London. The STL type, launched in 1932, which became the standard London double-decker of the period, was a huge advance on the open top, solid-tyred buses of ten years earlier.

Motor buses were cheaper to run than trams and far more flexible. Unlike trams they did not require any fixed infrastructure and could be steered round obstacles in the street. The bus network continued to expand, although in the 1930s it complemented the heavily used tram system rather than offering a viable alternative to it.

In 1931 the first electric trolleybuses replaced trams on some suburban routes in south west London. A trolleybus is a cross between a tram and a bus, electrically powered through overhead wires but not confined to rails in the road. Successful operating experience with this hybrid system soon led to trolleybuses being selected over motor buses for the wholesale conversion of London's huge tram network.

The most significant spur to progress on the streets in the 1930s was the creation of London Transport (LT). After years of debate but little action a single public transport authority was established by the government in July 1933. The London Passenger Transport Board (LPTB) became responsible for running all bus, tram and Underground railway services over a vast urban and country area across and around Greater London. At a time when very few people owned a car, the LPTB had to plan for the transport needs of more than nine million residents.

THIS MUST HAVE SEEMED LIKE A GOLDEN AGE ON THE BUSES

Buses were the most important part of London Transport's operations, and the only section of the organisation that was profitable, effectively cross-subsidising essential tram and Underground services. The LPTB was expected to cover its operating costs through fares, but could borrow the capital required for its ambitious modernisation programme. This involved expansion of the Underground and replacing the entire tram network with trolleybuses, both of which progressed rapidly during 1935–40.

For Londoners this must have seemed like a golden age on the buses. A growing fleet of modern, bright red vehicles criss-crossed central London and the suburbs, with green buses and coaches running far out into London's country. Staff and services were smart and efficient, and the very reasonable penny a mile fares never went up. It couldn't last.

Just before the Coronation of George VI in 1937, London Transport busmen went on strike for better wages and conditions. Two years later, when the LPTB was about to increase bus fares for the first time as costs escalated, a much more serious event intervened. From 3 September 1939 Britain was at war and London's bus services took on new roles in the national emergency.

This 'Whitsuntide' poster, 1931, was produced to promote bus excursions into London's country for sport and leisure. Open top double deck buses had virtually disappeared from regular service in London by this time even on country routes but they contribute to an attractive repeating design. Dora Batty, the artist, was primarily a textile designer and taught at the Central School of Arts & Crafts. When London Transport took over all services in 1933, dark green became the standard livery colour for all LT country buses.

1983/4/3107

Poster by Frances Halsted encouraging hikers to get out of town on the new Green Line coach services, 1932. Rambling was an increasingly popular and cheap leisure activity in the 1930s, encouraged by London Transport with its Country Walks booklets and the opening of youth hostels by the newly formed Youth Hostels Association (YHA).

1983/4/3383

Traffic at Marble Arch, 1930. The three
nearest buses demonstrate the rapid
design progress of the previous decade,
from the open top, solid tyred K type of
1919 (centre), through the first bus fitted
with a covered top, the NS type in 1925
(left) to the latest fully enclosed and
pneumatic tyred ST type of 1930 (right).
On the left a lone horseman braves the
busy motor traffic after a leisurely ride in
Hyde Park's Rotten Row.

1998/85521

A gleaming new ST type bus at Oxford Circus, 1930. Over 800 of these buses entered the LGOC fleet in 1930/31. The chassis and engines were built by AEC at their Southall plant in west London, where the bus was known as the Regent type. The bodies were designed, constructed and fitted at the LGOC's Chiswick Works. As well as being fully enclosed the ST had roller blind boxes instead of the removable wooden route and destination boards provided in the 1920s.

1998/79396

Traffic at Piccadilly Circus, summer 1932. The buses circling Eros are all open staircase NS types, soon to be replaced by a new generation of vehicles. There are also three single deck coaches to be seen at top right on private hire or long distance Green Line express services. Taxicabs still just outnumber private cars in the West End at this time. Invisible below the road is London Underground's latest marvel, the glamorous rebuilt Piccadilly Circus station, completed in 1928. One of the new subway entrances to the Tube is lower left.

2002/6503

By 1930 the LGOC was running most, but not all, of London's bus services. The largest of the remaining independent operators was Thomas Tilling, who purchased nearly 300 AEC Regents and built their own bodies for the new buses. As this 1931 view at Victoria shows, the Tilling Regent (on the left) with its outside staircase has a distinctively different appearance to the LGOC ST (right) built on the same chassis. Both fleets were taken over by London Transport when it was created two years later.

1998/78459

London and other British cities continued to favour the high capacity double deck bus as standard. Paris, by contrast, was only using single-deckers by the 1930s. The LGOC used single-deckers mainly for private hire work and as Green Line coaches. They were also introduced on lightly used or difficult suburban routes. One of the most challenging for buses in the 1930s was the long, steep gradient of Muswell Hill in north London. Crawling towards the top in this 1931 view is a newly built single deck Renown, classified an LTL type, but soon nicknamed the 'Scooter' by London bus crews.

1998/78435

Special bus services were laid on for the annual Derby Stakes at Epsom, running from Morden Tube station. A small fleet of old open-toppers was maintained by the LGOC for private hire. These buses were in particular demand on Derby Day as they could combine party transport to Epsom Downs with a grandstand view of the race and a private picnic enclosure on the top deck.

1998/54722

Photo montage poster by Maurice
Beck promoting the LGOC's impressive
'record of service' for 1931. During the
year its 4,754 buses had carried nearly
700m passengers over 185m route
miles. The main images feature a bus
driver and conductor, the uniformed
staff most obvious to passengers, while
the others show work behind the scenes
keeping London's buses on the move.
At a time of economic depression the
company was keen to stress that it was
a major employer as well as a service
provider, with more than 32,000 staff.

1983/4/3303

Buses at the Bank, August 1933. The Mansion House is on the left and the Bank of England on the far right in this view looking west from the roof of the Royal Exchange. This major road junction is at the heart of the City of London's financial district, and the streets are crowded, with at least twenty buses visible. The LPTB had come into being a few weeks earlier and acquired nearly 6,000 buses from the LGOC and independent operators, creating the largest single bus fleet in the world.

1998/85601

Elephant & Castle, 1933. This has always been one of south London's busiest road intersections, named after the large corner pub (top right). The only traffic control at this time appears to be a single policeman on point duty, who is standing in front of the removals van on the right. There are just two private cars in view, but the junction is already getting snarled up by a combination of buses, trams and goods vehicles crossing in different directions. Removing the trams and reconstructing this whole area with a massive roundabout after the war did not solve the congestion problem.

1998/85227

Seven Sisters Road outside Finsbury Park station during the evening rush hour, 1930. This photograph was taken to show the risk of accidents at the stop here as crowds scramble to board their tram home (left), walking out directly in front of cars and bikes. Buses were able to pull in safely close to the kerb to pick up but most lacked the carrying capacity to rival trams at this time. The nearest to the camera is one of the few that could, a big open cab London Six (LS type) bus, seating up to 72 passengers.

1998/79326

Press ad showing a map of the LPTB operating area established in July 1933. It covered nearly 2,000 square miles of the Greater London area and beyond in the Home Counties, with the outer boundaries of the traffic area some 30 miles from Charing Cross at Baldock in the north and Horsham in the south. The winged LPTB logo shown here lasted only a few months with a rapid reversion to the familiar bar and circle device with London Transport lettering.

2003/5392

The London Passenger Transport Board has assumed control of most of the passenger transport undertakings which operate in an area within a radius of some 30 miles from Charing Cross. The services include the underground railways, tramways, omnibuses and coaches.

2. The Territory

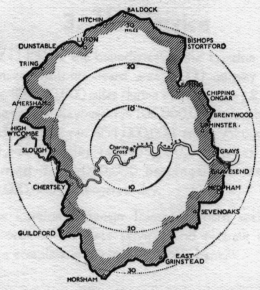

The area comprises 2,000 square miles, and the railway, tramway, omnibus and coach services which operate within its boundaries cater for a population of 9,000,000 people.

For all inquiries

LONDON PASSENGER TRANSPORT BOARD
55, Broadway, Westminster, S.W.1

Telephone: VICtoria 6800   Telegrams: Passengers Sowest London

This is No. 2 of a series of four announcements by the London Passenger Transport Board. Other announcements will be published at fortnightly intervals as follows:
3. The Service.   4. The Staff.

Moving or replacing tram track caused huge disruption, particularly in the LCC area where there was conduit track, and turned opinion against trams in the 1930s. This view of Shoreditch High Street in 1934 with a tram inching slowly over newly installed trackwork shows the advantage and flexibility of the bus, sailing past in the other direction towards Kingsland Road and Hackney. Trams did at least have fixed stopping points whereas buses could still in theory be hailed like a cab.

2003/18129

London's first trolleybuses, offering a flexible and almost silent alternative to the trams, were introduced in the south west suburbs from 1931. They were soon known as 'Diddlers'. Their big advantage was that they could be steered like a motor bus, as demonstrated here outside Wimbledon Town Hall in 1933. A 'Diddler' has arrived at the terminus of trolleybus route 4 and is about to turn back to Hampton Court via Kingston. A single deck 'Scooter' motor bus is passing on the left.

1999/20521

How to put up a bus stop, Watford 1934. London Transport created a complete network of fixed stops over a three year period. This is one of the last Birmingham Guild style cast iron poles formerly purchased by the LGOC in the 1920s from a manufacturer in the Midlands. The LPTB was soon mass-producing its own concrete posts at its works depot in Parsons Green and replacing the 'tombstone' shaped flags used since the early 1920s.

2003/18049

Waiting for the bus on the main Cambridge Road through Edmonton, north London, 1934. A new LPTB shelter, designed by the Underground's consulting architect Charles Holden, has been placed alongside a concrete GPO telephone box in front of a large new 'roadhouse' style pub, which is nearing completion. These are all characteristic features of London's fast developing suburban landscape at the time.

1998/69653

Morden Underground station, 1934, eight years after it opened on a green field site at the south western edge of London. The open countryside around the station has already been covered with semi-detached houses as far as the eye can see. Bus services were quickly developed as feeders to the Underground, bringing commuters in from further afield, turning more of Surrey into suburbia and making Morden the busiest outer Underground terminus.

1998/89403

A standard STL double-decker at a
newly installed bus stop in Hanwell,
west London, 1939. Hans Schleger
designed the classic rectangular bus
stop flag for London Transport in the
mid-1930s. He used the familiar bar and
circle logo in black and red on white at
compulsory stops like this, with white
on red for request stops and a green flag
at coach stops. London bus stops have
followed Schleger's distinctive design
ever since.

1998/85614
1995/2258

The body shop at Chiswick Works, with NS and LT type buses undergoing their annual service and maintenance, 1934. The bodies have been removed from their chassis and the mainly wooden frames and panelwork are being renovated on production lines. Each chassis was overhauled on another line next door before re-assembly. Work was becoming increasingly mechanised at Chiswick but it was also skilled and labour intensive, with more than 3,000 employees on site by this time, ranging from bus engineers to draughtsmen.

1998/50366

Trainee bus conductors at Chiswick, 1935, all wearing their smart new navy blue uniforms with silver buttons featuring the LPTB griffin emblem. Their peak caps have an enamel bulls-eye badge in blue and white with London Transport in silver lettering on the bar. The white cotton cap tops were for summer wear only.

1999/19993
2002/2791

The famous Chiswick skid pan with a group of hopeful bus drivers about to be tested on an old solid tyred NS type, 1934. None of the men are in uniform, so presumably they have not yet been taken on. Bus driving is a responsible job, and London Transport ensured that the highest standards were maintained through rigorous training and testing of their staff as well as annual safe driving awards (bottom right).

1998/46443
2004/9053

Bus crew in winter uniform, 1935. Their bus has no heating and although the cab is enclosed it has no door, so the driver wears a long, heavy overcoat. It was a strict rule that both crew members always had to wear their individually numbered licence badge visibly on their lapel. The white bands on their cuffs are to help when giving hand signals. The conductor carries a wooden rack with tickets in a different colour for each fare value. He will use his Bell Punch and leather cash bag every time he issues a ticket from the rack to a passenger.

1998/36915

To promote better standards of safety on the roads, The Royal Society for the Prevention of Accidents invited bus drivers to voluntarily take annual assessments. If successful, they were given Safe Driving Awards, identified by medals such as this example from 1931.

2004/9053

Buses lined up for service in Upton Park garage, West Ham, 1933. This was then the largest bus garage in east London. Nearly 1,500 of these LT type buses were in service when London Transport took over from the LGOC. By 1940 all of them had been converted from petrol to diesel engines. This was found to save up to £120 a year in fuel costs per bus and all new LPTB bus orders after 1933 were for diesel, or oil engines as they were called at the time.

1998/63324

A dramatic 1935 air-brushed modernist poster by Tom Eckersley and Eric Lombers encouraging Londoners to use the bus when they went out to the cinema. Large new super-cinemas opened all over London in the 1930s and going out to 'the pictures' became the most popular form of leisure entertainment.

1983/4/9728

BY BUS TO THE PICTURES TO-NIGHT

A wet evening in Regent Street 1935, looking towards Piccadilly Circus. It is crowded with at least a dozen buses but very little other traffic. This is close to many of the main West End cinemas, theatres and shops. As tramways had never been allowed in the City or the West End except along the Embankment and through the Kingsway subway, both these central areas remained bus dominated and free from trolleybuses as they progressively replaced trams in the 1930s.

2004/19858

A size comparison of the latest London Transport road vehicles in Chiswick High Road, 1937. From left to right the single deck T type Green Line coach has 30 seats, the double deck STL type bus 56 and the standard trolleybus 70, showing why trolleys were chosen instead of buses for one to one tram replacement. Trams had disappeared completely from the western suburbs by this time. Between 1935 and 1940 the trolleybus system grew from just 18 route miles to 255, while the tramways shrank to 102 route miles.

1998/85160

Cover of a London Transport 'Pleasure Outings' booklet showing the huge chalk lion cut into the Chiltern downs near Dunstable in 1933. The lion marks the location of Whipsnade, the new 'country branch' of London Zoo, which had opened nearby. At a time when few people owned a car, the green country bus or coach was the only way that most Londoners could get to Whipsnade, which was right at the northern edge of the LPTB area in Bedfordshire. It was the first limited stop service by Green Line coach, direct from Baker Street in 1932.

1995/625

Detail from a folding Green Line brochure designed by Laszlo Moholy-Nagy in 1937. The express coach services had expanded rapidly since 1930 and are promoted here with London Transport's usual sophisticated style. The leaflet has gushing diary notes by 'Irene Glen', a fashionable Home Counties lady who enthuses about going by comfortable, luxury coach to various places in town on shopping, lunch and theatre trips. Her name is of course an anagram of Green Line.

Oliver Green collection

Poster advertising London Transport guided coach tours, 1937. The coach shown is a Q type, an ingenious Chiswick design with the engine re-positioned from the front to the off-side of the vehicle behind the driver. There were single deck bus and coach variants of this innovative vehicle and even five experimental double-deckers with the entrance at the front, which looked very much like modern buses built since the 1960s.

1983/4/4838

Transition at King's Cross, June 1938. Three buses are heading away from the camera towards St Pancras. In the foreground a newly introduced trolleybus is crossing from Caledonian Road towards Holborn, running over the conduit tram track which will soon be redundant. Trolleybuses are also about to replace trams along Pentonville Road here. The overhead wiring is in place, with a support pole prominent on the corner of the street. Route 30 still runs here today after both trams and trolleybuses are long gone.

1998/44117

A round London guided tour in Parliament Square, Westminster. The coach is a new TF type, the first to have an underfloor engine allowing more seating and in this case panoramic roof windows for better sightseeing. Just two weeks after this publicity shot was taken on 14 August 1939, war was declared. The tour service was suspended and the coaches were put into store. All but one were subsequently destroyed by enemy action. The Green Line TFs were converted to ambulances for the duration of the war.

1998/44344

10

War and austerity – the 1940s

Oliver Green

There had been no civilian preparations for war in 1914. Twenty five years later, the radio announcement to the nation on 3 September 1939 by Prime Minister Neville Chamberlain that 'this country is at war with Germany' came as no great surprise. For more than a year Hitler's aggressive stance towards Nazi Germany's European neighbours had threatened to plunge the Continent into chaos. By September 1938, when the Munich crisis arose, London Transport had prepared detailed defence plans which would allow it to remain operational should the capital come under aerial bombardment, the greatest fear of the time. In fact the 'Blitz' air raids on London did not begin until 1940, which at least allowed more physical defences to be developed.

Two days before the official declaration of war in 1939, plans for the mass evacuation of the city were put in place. Over four days nearly half a million people, mainly children and expectant mothers, were conveyed out of London by bus and train. Hospital patients were removed by Green Line coaches swiftly converted into temporary ambulances.

Blackout restrictions were applied immediately and London Transport's petrol and oil supplies were cut by 25 per cent as an economy measure. Bus services were reduced or withdrawn altogether to save fuel and within four months more than 800 red buses were lying idle. Some Green Line coach services were restored and the last tram-to-trolleybus conversion in east London was completed by June 1940.

The German Air Force (Luftwaffe) began its devastating mass raids on 7 September, and London was bombed heavily every night until 2 November 1940, after which the Blitz continued intermittently until May 1941. In 57 raids on the city more than 15,000 civilians were killed and many more made homeless. Over 200 LT road vehicles were destroyed by enemy action and many more were badly damaged.

Disruption to the London Transport system was severe but never crippling. A service of some kind could nearly always be maintained: buses could easily be diverted, whilst continued operation was more difficult on the tram and Underground systems when trackwork and tunnels were hit. London Transport kept the capital going through six difficult years of war, when civilians and military personnel were both carried and sheltered across the city.

LONDON TRANSPORT KEPT LONDON GOING THROUGH SIX DIFFICULT YEARS OF WAR

London Transport also made a major contribution to the war effort through its workshops, building bomber aircraft instead of new buses and preparing tanks and landing craft for the invasion of Europe. Much of this vital work was done by newly recruited women who had little or no previous engineering experience.

When the war ended in 1945 it had taken a considerable toll on staff and services. Air raids had killed 426 road and rail staff, with nearly 3,000 injured. A vast amount of repair work to London Transport's bombed or neglected infrastructure was necessary and there was a desperate shortage of buses at a time when passenger numbers were at an all time high and still growing. Reconstruction began almost immediately but it was clear that a long period of post-war austerity lay ahead.

Goodbye Hitler. Schoolchildren are
evacuated from the city by bus,
1 September 1939. Many evacuees
were transferred to main line trains to
complete their journeys from central
London to the safety of the countryside.
In four days more than half a million
people were conveyed out of the danger
zone by bus, coach, tram, trolleybus or
Underground train.

9098/8622

On 1 September 1939 all Green Line coaches were withdrawn. Within five hours 400 of them had been converted into temporary ambulances to evacuate London's hospitals. Each coach could carry up to ten patients on stretchers. This was a remarkable exercise on a very large scale, and successfully completed by the time war was declared two days later.

1998/52664

Take cover! Air raid sirens went off a few minutes after the Prime Minister's radio announcement of war on 3 September 1939. It turned out to be a false alarm, but these two bus drivers are taking a cycling policeman's warning seriously and abandoning their empty buses. In fact air attacks on London did not start until a year later in the summer of 1940.

1998/37697

Cartoonist David Langdon came up with Billy Brown of London Town, an annoying little man in a bowler hat who gave advice to his fellow commuters about sensible behaviour in the wartime blackout. These ditties in rhyming couplets appeared on posters in buses, soon attracting graffiti responses from the travelling public when the conductor wasn't looking.

1983/4/5426

Billy Brown of London Town

Billy Brown's own highway Code
For blackouts is 'Stay off the Road'.
He'll never step out and begin
To meet a bus that's pulling in.
He doesn't wave his torch at night,
But 'flags' his bus with something white.
He never jostles in a queue,
But waits and takes his turn. Do you?

Printed for
London ⊕ Transport

Everyone was encouraged to save paper in wartime. The size and thickness of bus tickets was reduced and waste paper was pulped for re-use. London Transport showed it had a sense of humour by reprinting this witty Fougasse cartoon from *Punch* magazine in 1940 as a small panel poster inside buses.

1983/4/10461

By special permission of the Proprietors of PUNCH

"Stop! Stop!! I forgot to put my ticket in your litterbox!!!"

Help us save paper ⊕

One of six portraits of London Transport staff by official war artist Eric Kennington issued as morale boosting posters in 1944. Each individual was selected because he or she had made a special contribution to keeping London safely on the move under attack. This is Mrs M J Morgan, a conductor from Athol Street garage in Poplar, who had been quietly heroic when her bus was caught in an air raid. She protected four children on board by quickly bundling them under the seats.

1983/4/5688

SEEING IT THROUGH

How proud upon your quarterdeck you stand,
  Conductor—Captain—of the mighty bus!
Like some Columbus you survey the Strand,
  A calm newcomer in a sea of fuss.

You may be tired—how cheerfully you clip,
  Clip in the dark, with one eye on the street;
Two decks—one pair of legs—a rolling ship—
  Much on your mind—and fat men on your feet!

The sirens blow, and death is in the air:
  Still at her post the trusty Captain stands,
And counts her change, and scampers up the stair,
  As brave a sailor as the King commands.

A. P. Herbert

A gas attack exercise in Esher, 1941. There was a general fear that London might be targeted with gas bombs, and all civilians were supposed to carry their gas masks with them at all times. Fortunately gas was never used but the authorities were anxious that everyone was prepared for this eventuality. Wartime bus tickets carried little reminders on the reverse about not leaving your gas mask on the bus.

1998/36455
2003/4120

160 London buses were converted to run on producer gas, generated in special anthracite-burning trailer units towed behind each vehicle, as seen here at Green Park, Piccadilly in 1941. The idea was to save petrol, which it did, but the producer gas buses were slow and unreliable, and the experiment ended once the supply of imported fuel improved.

1998/89507

Enjoy your War Work. As in the First World War, women were taken on for many transport jobs, but in much greater numbers and in a wider range of roles. Mabel Notley, who was photographed for this recruitment poster in 1941, was a shop assistant at Bentall's department store in Kingston before joining London Transport to become a wartime 'clippie'.

2003/13125

All buses had masked headlamps and reduced interior lighting, making evening travel in the blackout hazardous for passengers and difficult for drivers. London Transport's wartime posters were more about safety than publicity. This typical example by Bruce Angrave appeared in 1942.

1983/4/5552

'They also serve' was one of a poster series celebrating the contribution of unseen staff working behind the scenes in depots and garages, 1944. The strapline 'Back room boys' is a little ironic, as two of the three workers servicing a bus in Fred Taylor's central illustration are women. The background image shows a trolleybus depot.

1983/4/5576

'BACK ROOM BOYS'

BUS MAINTENANCE

'THEY ALSO SERVE'

From the start of the Blitz on
7 September 1940 London was bombed
every night for seven weeks. Bus
services continued to run throughout,
but with heavy disruption on a daily
basis. 'Road spotter' inspectors were
posted at key locations looking for
trouble, planning diversions and pointing
them out to drivers on the streets, as
here in October 1940. With no radio
control, this was a demanding task.
1998/53229

Regional cities lent buses to London
to replace bomb damaged vehicles
which could not be repaired. This is
a Manchester Corporation bus being
fitted with London Transport blinds to
work route 13 across the centre of the
capital, October 1940.
1998/43322

More buses were lost in the Blitz when garages were hit in night bombing raids than out on the streets. These four STLs were burnt out and destroyed by fire after Croydon garage was hit by incendiaries in May 1941. Camberwell, Catford and Clapham bus garages were all badly damaged in separate Blitz attacks in 1940/41.

1998/75612

Did y
MACL
your feet

2002/9811

One of the most familiar images of London at war is the double-decker bus blown into a huge crater when a high explosive bomb hit Balham High Street on 14 October 1940. The bus had no passengers at the time and the driver and conductor were thrown clear and unhurt. However, 68 people sheltering in the Tube station below were killed when burst water mains flooded the tunnels after the blast. As a result of the bomb, shops and tramlines in the street above the station were destroyed, and the wrecked LT type bus could only be removed with a crane two weeks later.

2002/9811
1998/27688

With AEC fully occupied on war work, London Transport was eventually able to acquire a limited number of new 'utility' buses from other manufacturers. This is a Guy Arab built in Wolverhampton, on LT service at Golders Green, north London, in 1943. The utility buses had extremely spartan interiors, some with slatted wooden seats, quite a contrast to the comfortable pre-war seat cushions covered in woollen moquette.

1998/89499
1998/75679

Soldiers and civilians in a long queue outside Sidcup garage, south east London, October 1943. The worst of the Blitz was over by May 1941, but even though the threat of air raids had diminished, a wartime bus journey was often slow, uncomfortable and disrupted. By 1944 London was under attack again from unmanned flying bombs. A V1 rocket which hit Elmers End garage in Bromley on 18 July 1944 killed ten London Transport staff and destroyed several buses.

1998/43636

Converted Green Line coaches were painted grey and used as 'Clubmobiles' by the American Red Cross. These provided mobile canteen and welfare services to the growing number of US troops and airmen on bases in England from 1942 onwards. The Clubmobiles appeared in a series of free Red Cross postcards for US troops to send back home (below). These postcards are unusual in that some feature black Americans at a time when US military units were effectively segregated.

1998/20590
2001/13320

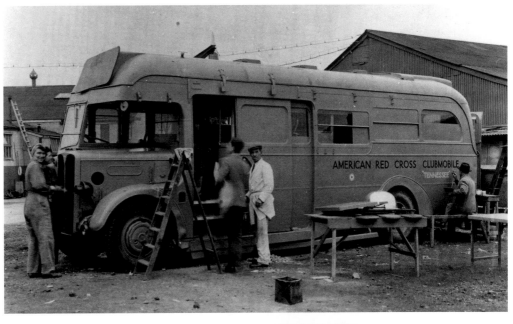

The war years were not entirely free of labour disputes. In April 1943 12,000 London busmen took strike action and during the stoppage only a very limited bus service was provided by army personnel using military vehicles. This extremely basic open 'lorry bus' was photographed picking up passengers somewhere in Hackney.

1998/63168

The Victory Parade in the Mall, 8 June 1946. London Transport entered a pair of RT types, its final pre-war bus design, seen here passing King George VI and Queen Elizabeth, with The Queen Mother, on the royal dais. Only 150 RTs had been completed when production was suspended in 1940 because of the conflict and as yet no new buses had been delivered in the first twelve months of peace.

1998/35717

'Rehabilitation…it takes time'. Another poster by Fred Taylor issued after May 1945, which is self-explanatory. London Transport was well aware that it faced an uphill task in peacetime and with the financial constraints of the immediate post-war period there could not be a rapid return to the 'normal' conditions of the 1930s.

1983/4/5811

'Avoid peak period congestion by staggering working hours'. This poster by Beverly Pick in 1947 was part of a major campaign by London Transport in the late 1940s as bus use shot up, but it seemed to be aiming at the wrong target. Most workers had little choice or control over their working hours and this idea would have been better addressed to employers. Flexible work time was simply not on their agenda and rush hour congestion got worse.

1983/4/10620

The new approved post-war colour scheme for red central area double-deckers shown on an RT type. This is taken from a book of hand painted drawings prepared at Chiswick Works c1946. The pre-war red with a wide white upper and lower deck window band was replaced by all over red and a narrow cream/yellow band above the lower deck windows. The improved version of the RT, with standard interchangeable parts, began to arrive from 1947 to be painted in these colours.

1998/36734

REHABILITATION

59,750 windows in trains, buses, trolleybuses and trams were damaged by enemy action, apart from those on totally blitzed vehicles. The wartime substitutes are being replaced by glass—but

IT TAKES TIME

Avoid peak period congestion

by staggering working hours

ARRANGEMENT OF 56 SEATER DOUBLE DECK BUS. Approved Colour Scheme.

London Transport's road services were carrying more passengers than ever before in the late 1940s. Where trolleybuses had replaced trams on the main roads of north London, the big 70-seat vehicles were particularly effective at clearing Saturday football crowds, which were also at a peak. This is Tottenham High Road after a Spurs home game in 1948, with at least 15 trolleys hoovering up the fans. Only ten years later diesel buses would begin to replace trolleybuses.

1998/76711

Bomb damaged London hosted the first post-war Olympic Games in 1948, known inevitably as the 'Austerity Olympics'. The athletes were housed in basic army Nissen huts and airfields at locations like RAF Uxbridge and bussed in each day to the main Olympic venue at Wembley Stadium. London Transport produced its first special post-war map and guide to assist overseas visitors.

1998/44575
1986/69/4

Traffic scene in Regent Street, 1949, with continuing signs of austerity four years after the end of the war. The bus in the centre is one of the wartime utility vehicles. It is flanked by two pre-war STLs. All three still have their muddy brown painted roofs, which had replaced the pre-war silver livery to make them less conspicuous from the air. The buses also retain their wartime economy reduced destination blinds. The London taxi in the foreground is a pre-war Austin Low-loader.

1998/85413

As vehicle shortages in the capital continued after the war, provincial operators came to London Transport's assistance again. This is a Bristol low bridge bus on loan from Hants & Dorset, carrying a temporary roundel on the radiator while on LT service at Ilford in 1949. In the background is one of the newly delivered post-war RT type buses, which were at last coming on stream.

2010/23297 photo by C Carter

11

Recovery and congestion— the 1950s

Oliver Green

London Transport was nationalised in 1948, becoming the London Transport Executive (LTE), a single division of the newly created British Transport Commission, which was also responsible for British Railways. Under direct government financial control, and lacking the dynamic pre-war leadership of Lord Ashfield and Frank Pick, the LTE struggled to find a way forward. It was carrying more road and rail passengers in the late 1940s than ever before, but did not have the resources to properly complete its pre-war modernisation plans. Housing, the new National Health Service and rebuilding other key industries took priority over London's transport needs.

Large orders were placed with both AEC and Leyland for an improved post-war version of London Transport's RT type bus but the rate of delivery was slow. Worn out pre-war vehicles were being withdrawn from service faster than new buses could be introduced. Partly as a result of their flexibility demonstrated during the disruptions of the war, it had already been decided to use new diesel buses rather than trolleybuses to complete the tram replacement programme. Remaining tram routes were closed down between 1950 and 1952, and there were no further extensions to the trolleybus network, which was also replaced by buses from 1958-62.

Unable to persuade the government to invest in the huge capital costs of new Underground railway projects in the 1950s, London Transport concentrated its limited resources on research and development, particularly in bus engineering. The fleet of RT type double-deckers grew to nearly 7,000 more or less standard vehicles and a huge new bus works was created at Aldenham, where every bus was sent for a regular overhaul. In 1954 the prototype Routemaster (RM) bus was unveiled, an advanced diesel bus developed by London Transport to replace the trolleybus. Its unique combination of robust practicality and elegant styling were to make the RM a much loved and long lived icon of the city. But as the production models entered service from 1959, LT was facing new problems on the streets.

Since the late 1940s peak, passenger use of the red Central area services had been in almost continuous decline, for reasons largely outside London Transport's control. The reduction in off-peak leisure travel was particularly marked, as domestic habits changed. Sales and rentals of television sets went up, particularly for the Queen's Coronation in 1953 and again after the introduction of a second tv channel in 1955. Londoners were staying in with their new home entertainment rather than going out by bus.

LONDON TRANSPORT HAD THE BEST AND MOST COMFORTABLE BUSES IN THE WORLD

Car ownership in London increased rapidly once wartime petrol rationing finally ended in 1950, and more than doubled in the next ten years. This private motoring boom was a double problem for London Transport as it meant fewer passengers and poorer bus services because of growing traffic congestion. The population of Greater London began to decline anyway after the war, though in London Transport's country area it grew steadily with a strong demand for bus and coach services in the New Towns developed beyond the Green Belt.

As the 1960s began, London Transport had the best and most comfortable buses in the world. But traffic congestion, staff shortages and unreliable service schedules seemed to be conspiring to bring them to a regular standstill.

This 1958 poster by Peter Roberson was commissioned to promote the new Red Rover ticket, which offered a day's unlimited travel on central buses and could take you to all these London landmarks for five shillings (around £5 in 2014).In the same year London busmen went on strike for seven weeks, which only encouraged the steady decline in passenger numbers. London Transport still had the best buses in the world but seemed unable to address its growing operational problems in the city.
1983/4/6974

In the summer of 1950, four new RT type buses were sent on a 4,000 mile, four month tour of continental Europe to promote the 1951 Festival of Britain. Here two of the Festival buses are being loaded on to a cargo vessel in the London Docks for the tour. They were back on the streets of London when the Festival opened on the South Bank the following year (below). The only permanent feature to remain on the site was the Royal Festival Hall. All the other innovative structures designed for the South Bank exhibition such as the Skylon and Dome of Discovery were demolished when it closed.

1998/21489
1998/21070

Following the success of the Festival of Britain, London Transport effectively became the capital's official visitor promoter at a time when no tourist board existed for the city. This distinctive 1952 poster, advertising the expanded bus and coach tour programme, is by Abram Games, who had designed the famous Festival symbol. The first edition of *Visitor's London*, a handy pocket guide to the city's sights with details of how to get there by bus and Underground, was published by LT in 1954.

1983/4/6544
1996/3183

Two Green Line drivers and a conductress at Windsor garage admiring their first newly allocated RF type coach, 1951. The AEC Regal Four (RF) had an underfloor engine and front entrance, with bodywork styled by industrial designer Douglas Scott, who was later to work on the Routemaster. The RF became LT's standard but flexible single deck workhorse of the 1950s, with design adaptations for use as a bus or coach with or without a folding powered door.

1998/72396

Lightly used country routes, especially those that served remote villages in the Home Counties, were still handled by small pre-war buses in 1950. These were all replaced in 1953/4 with the delivery of 84 26-seat GS type single-deckers, which were suitable for driver-only operation without a conductor. Although the Guy Specials were not strictly a London Transport design, these popular little buses had the most pleasing and elegant styling ever seen on an LT vehicle.

1998/83757

Replacement of the remaining tram network with buses rather than trolleybuses started in 1950. This is the first RT type bus to run out of the former Wandsworth tram depot over the now disused tracks at the garage entrance, September 1950. Most of the new buses entering service initially carried no commercial advertising at this time.

1998/87141

The last tram routes were replaced by diesel buses in July 1952. Each tram announced its own fate during last tram week and special tickets were issued to all tram passengers in the final days. The demise of London's trams was recorded in a poignant and elegaic documentary by British Transport Films called *The Elephant Will Never Forget*, shown in cinemas from 1953. At the time London Transport would have preferred a promotion of its future with buses.

1998/44244

Stockwell bus garage was the most
impressive piece of new architecture
completed for London Transport in
the 1950s. Steel was in short supply
at the time and the architects Adie
Button and Partners came up with an
ingenious roof design using reinforced
concrete arches instead to create a
massive uninterrupted covered space.
The spectacular roof dwarfs the buses
housed there in this 1953 view. It is still
used as a bus garage today and is now a
listed building.

2005/12517

Two RT type buses crossing London Bridge, June 1952. Six months later Tower Bridge, seen in the distance, was the scene of a lucky escape for another London bus. On 30 December the bridge bascules suddenly began to rise just as a double-decker on route 78 was crossing. With no time to stop, driver Albert Gunter accelerated and his bus jumped the gap that was opening up. Nobody on board was seriously hurt and driver Gunter was given a £10 reward for his bravery and quick thinking.
1998/85514

Winter London by Molly Moss, 1950. A colourful London Transport poster showing happy crowds out for Christmas shows and shopping by bus in Piccadilly Circus,
1983/4/6367

The reality of post-war London was that it was still a grey and unglamorous city of bombsites, rationing and austerity at the start of the fifties but there were soon efforts to brighten up the West End. Christmas lights and decorations were first put up all down Regent Street in 1954 in what became an eagerly anticipated seasonal celebration, later extended to Oxford Street. Today the lights are still best viewed from the top of a bus.

1998/85409

Xmas?
Biro
PADDINGTON
OXFORD CIRCUS
CHARING CROSS
BANK ALDGATE
POPLAR
15
EAST HAM WHITE HORSE
15
ST. JOHNS WOOD
CHARING CROSS
KENNINGTON
BRIXTON
NORBURY
59A
ADDISCOMBE
59A
KEEP

Victoria bus station, 1953. All but one of the 18 buses seen here are from the post-war RT family delivered since 1947, which had given London Transport its largest ever standardised fleet of double deck vehicles. When the final RT was built in the following year this amounted to nearly 7,000 buses, allowing LT to replace the last of its ageing pre-war vehicles.

1998/89074

Portrait of an RT in front of the Horse Guards in Whitehall c1956. The post-war RT3 construction incorporated some of the valuable lessons learnt by LT bus engineers who had set up London Aircraft Production (LAP) to build Halifax bombers during the war. Interchangeable parts and assembly on jigs meant a large number of identical units could be built quickly and that they were simple to service. The next London bus design, the Routemaster, would take these principles further but far fewer were needed.

2002/19059

To maintain the huge RT fleet, London Transport built an enormous bus overhaul works at Aldenham in Hertfordshire, completed in 1956. The site was originally to be used for a new Underground railway depot on the Northern line extension from Edgware to Bushey Heath, planned in the 1930s but abandoned after the war. The depot had been used for Halifax bomber assembly but was rebuilt and massively expanded with a long, double height main hall where bodies and chassis could be separated for overhaul using overhead gantry cranes. Each bus in the fleet went through Aldenham every three or four years, and to the confusion of bus spotters emerged looking brand new but with identical bodies and chassis often swapped around in the process. Who could tell?

2004/16146
1998/86151

Thick fog, sometimes turning into industrial smog, was still a regular winter feature of 1950s London, made worse by coal fires and general air pollution. Bus services could be badly disrupted and in extreme cases of reduced visibility inspectors had to guide buses at walking pace holding a burning wax flare. This is an RTL on the 96 edging its way through fog towards Aldgate in 1956, somewhere in central London.

1998/75614

An ingenious roll ticket machine designed by George Gibson, superintendent of the LT ticket works in Brixton, was introduced in 1953. Over the next five years these replaced Bell Punches on all central area buses and trolleybuses. The Gibson was a heavy machine that had to be worn on a harness. The conductor could set a dial and turn the handle to print off a ticket to any fare value on the blank ticket roll carried inside. It was a feature of London buses used for forty years until 1993.

1998/87163
1998/71077

The most serious difficulty facing London Transport in the 1950s was a shortage of bus operating staff. From 1951 the wartime policy of engaging women as conductors was resumed. At a time of full employment when office and factory jobs were easy to find, the unsocial hours and shift work required on the buses was not very appealing to young Londoners of either sex. In 1956 London Transport tried a new policy of direct recruitment overseas, signing up staff from Ireland, Malta and, in particular, the West Indies. Caribbean recruitment started in Barbados, where LT Personnel Officer Charles Gomm is seen signing up young men for employment thousands of miles from home.

1998/83757

One of the early arrivals in 1957 was Ralph Straker, photographed in his first LT job as a trolleybus conductor at Finchley depot with his Scottish driver Laurie Herridle.

1998/18597

A high point for London buses in the fifties is shown in this shot of traffic in Trafalgar Square. It was taken on Coronation Day, 2 June 1953, as crowds make their way home after watching the Queen's procession to Westminster Abbey. There were 44,000 bus journeys in central London that day and buses are queuing as far as the eye can see.

1998/85373

A low point for London buses, this view of Trafalgar Square five years after the Coronation also shows traffic at a standstill, at 9am on the first day of the 1958 bus strike. There is a black cab in the foreground, a motorcycle and a sea of private cars, with not a single bus on the streets. Daily use of the red buses continued to decline and fell even more sharply after the seven week strike.

1998/89452

While use of the red central area buses declined, there was a growing demand for London Transport's green country bus and coach services in the 1950s and early 1960s. This was driven in particular by the first generation of New Towns established after the war beyond London's green belt at Crawley, Harlow, Hatfield/Welwyn, Hemel Hempstead and Stevenage, which were all planned for public transport. Most of the early residents were former Londoners and in the early days very few of them had a car. This view shows a green RT on a new housing estate in Stevenage in 1957.
1998/88412

'Please avoid the rush hours' poster by Victor Galbraith, 1959. London Transport's publicity seemed to be more about putting off its regular customers than finding solutions to peak hour overcrowding. The bus became a slow and frustrating way to get to work in central London.
1983/4/7055

London Transport's marketing strategy for country buses and Green Line remained entirely geared to leisure travel and the Londoner looking for a day out. There was little attempt to promote the new local services outside Greater London to the rising number of country area residents. LT's well established standards of high quality posters and maps were maintained, but they had little impact on passenger numbers. This example from 1961 is typical: an attractive poster for Green Rover tickets by Edward Robert Bartelt.
1983/4/7243

The prototype Routemaster, 'London's bus of the future', was built in 1954. RM1 was rigorously tested for two years before entering trial public service on route 2 in February 1956, chosen because it then ran right across London from Golders Green to Crystal Palace. Six months later RM1 featured on the cover of the *Meccano Magazine*, the popular engineering journal for boys.

2004/17903

The second Routemaster prototype, RM2, was initially painted green and trialled on country route 406. It is seen here at Tattenham Corner, Epsom in 1957 showing the second stage of RM front end design with a grille over the radiator. The two original RM prototypes remained experimental vehicles and various features were changed and adapted over the years. Both are now preserved in London Transport Museum's collection and RM2 has been returned to its original green appearance.

1998/87344

Production of the Routemaster by AEC started in 1958. The traditional appearance and layout of the bus, with a half cab and open rear platform, disguised its radical engineering and construction. The RM has a metal frame body built by Park Royal Vehicles with a 'stressed skin' which does not require a heavy chassis to give it structural strength. The use of aluminium alloy throughout made a large 64-seat bus lighter than the 56-seat RT, and saved fuel. It was easy to drive, with automatic transmission and a ride quality equivalent to most saloon cars in the early 1960s.

2001/56652

Newly delivered Routemasters are prepared for their first day replacing trolleybuses from Poplar depot, November 1959. Behind them on the left and right are lines of redundant trolleybuses. This was the first conversion using RMs and in less than three years LT's road services were all handled by diesel buses. Electric trolleybus services in London ended in May 1962 at Fulwell Depot in the south west suburbs where they had started in 1931.

1998/87344

Finsbury Square, just outside the City of London boundary, was the turning point for trolleybus routes from the northern suburbs. This view was taken just before the end of trolleybus operation here in 1961. A new Routemaster bus is already in service on one route and can be seen in the background. As yet there are no yellow lines or other restrictions to worry the owner of the Ford Anglia parked in front of the trolleybus stop.

2011/6178

Buses, taxis and cars, including a new Mini, in Trafalgar Square,
1960. Early attempts by the planning authorities to deal with
traffic congestion caused by rising car use in central London
were limited to the introduction of parking restrictions and
meters. In the 1960s the car lobby got the upper hand and
there were major schemes for road widening and urban
motorways. Public transport and the bus in particular fell out
of fashion. All traffic was eventually removed from this road
outside the National Gallery when it was pedestrianised over
forty years later in 2003.

2002/18148

Rise of the private car and decline of the bus, 1960–79

Roger French

In the 1960s London was cool, fashionable, and the place to be: it was 'swinging'. Everything became much more colourful as the post war austerity was finally shaken off. On the high street a retail revolution began slowly as grocery chains became self-service shops and soon larger, much grander supermarkets became the norm. Influenced by the emergence of pop culture, fashion and style, people became 'consumers' and began enjoying shopping as a leisure activity, with a wider range of products and services offering greater choice and freedoms. London Transport's well-oiled bureaucracy, which had served well during its first thirty years, struggled to keep up with the pace of change as the decade progressed. The metamorphosis of the London Transport Executive into the London Transport Board in 1963, reporting directly to the Minister of Transport, was symptomatic of the need for greater investment in the capital's transport infrastructure, but for buses the priority became cost savings and efficiencies as passenger numbers fell.

The enduring transport icon of the sixties was undoubtedly the Routemaster bus which supplanted the last of the trolleybuses and provided increased capacity over older RT buses. By 1965, however, three years before the last Routemaster was introduced and as flirtations with front entrance buses started, it had already become operationally outdated. Driver-only operation began to expand, although at this time, not withstanding employment costs and entrenched trade union attitudes for their retention, conductors still dominated the scene. These staff became more difficult to recruit as the unsocial shift hours required became increasingly unattractive, at a time when society generally was moving to a more regular Monday to Friday, nine-to-five, working pattern.

Besides resourcing problems, the relentless growth of car ownership presented additional significant challenges during the 1960s. Many people now enjoyed a choice of travel mode and given the door-to-door convenience and relative ease of parking it was unsurprising that people readily chose their own vehicle rather than a bus. But private cars also led to chronic levels of congestion, with serious impacts on public transport journey times and service reliability.

The London County Council (LCC) was abolished in 1965, to be replaced by the Greater London Council (GLC) covering a larger geographical area. Both authorities believed the way to tackle increasing congestion was to pursue plans for large scale road building based on the 'Ringway' proposals first mooted by Sir Patrick Abercrombie in his plans of 1943 and 1944.[1] In west London, for example, the A40 Westway was built during 1964-70, and in 1969 the GLC produced the *Greater London Development Plan*, which included ambitious plans for roads and inner city motorways.[2] The bus was not seen as a viable solution to traffic congestion and received little priority.

The 1970s have been described as the party hangover after the idealism and expansion of the 1960s collapsed. Commentator Dominic Sandbrook observed that the decade marked a reckoning for a country that had been complacent for too long, basking in the sunshine of post-war affluence. Mired in a high level of inflation, industrial difficulties, picket lines, the 'three day week',[3] the 1974 oil crisis and the 'winter of discontent',[4]

they were difficult years for Britain both politically and economically. In London, many docks and factories closed, reflecting significant shifts in global trade. All of these national and local conditions negatively affected London's public transport.

The same observation appositely describes London's buses during the 1970s. London Transport's complacency in ordering and introducing a large fleet of Routemaster buses late into the 1960s came home to roost in the 1970s as it struggled to operate off-the-peg standard one-person operated (OPO) buses purchased in a hurry. Engineers hadn't been trained to maintain these buses and found it hard to keep enough on the road, despite such vehicles running perfectly well elsewhere.

PRIVATE CAR OWNERSHIP CHALLENGED BUS OPERATION IN THE 1960s

In 1970 the London Transport Board, operator of red buses and the Underground network in Greater London, and reporting directly to central government, was reconstituted as a London Transport Executive, answerable to the Greater London Council. This put the capital's buses directly under the control of local politicians, which in the long-term resulted in many improvements in organisation and infrastructure. Importantly, £270 million of debt, much still left over from the London Transport New Works Programme of 1935-40, was written off and a plan for spending £275 million over the next twenty years drawn up.[5]

Political influence over London Transport became more evident during the 1970s, because of direct control by the GLC. As political power at the Council changed hands, from left to right and back again, support for buses ebbed and flowed. Labour administrators broadly favoured public transport, whilst Conservatives advanced priorities for private motorists. This shifting commitment fragmented policy and practice for development of the bus network.[6]

Despite the country's economic challenges during the decade, disposable incomes and affluence continued to grow. Foreign holidays became commonplace, home furnishings and goods such as colour televisions became the norm. Conversely, bus passenger numbers continued to decline, as private car use and congestion increased further. London Transport had to run to catch up, often finding itself stumbling along the way. Cultural change came even faster than in the 1960s. By the end of the decade, however, Margaret Thatcher had become Britain's first woman Prime Minister. Jill Viner became the first female bus driver in 1974. The challenges of staff shortages and road crowding continued, as London Transport encountered new obstacles to progress in a lack of skilled maintenance workers, wrestling with variable mechanical reliability in vehicles which were unsuitable for the task of serving London. Transport managers had not faced up to the challenges of car ownership, staff shortages and engineering failure – creating a bus sevice which was unreliable, with falling passenger numbers.

The unmistakeable Routemaster, represented here by RM975 on route 276 in 1961, passing through Parliament Square with one of the capital's other internationally known landmarks the Palace of Westminster, in the background.
1999/20391

A typical early 1960s scene in the Strand looking west towards Admiralty Arch. Buses and other vehicles mix happily on the wide thoroughfare with enough space on the pavements for pedestrians, and no need yet for yellow road markings to control parking. The white LCC ambulance (foreground left) and a Post Office van (mid-ground centre) turning right into the Strand are typical of commercial vehicles of the time. We see a plentiful supply of RT type vehicles, including one bound for Bricklayers Arms on route 1.

1998/44798

The forecourt of Sudbury Town Underground station on the Piccadilly line in north-west London had parking space for just six cars in the 1960s. The 64 seats on the adjacent Routemaster offer far more capacity, particularly useful as route 16 was one of the busiest services, linking the area with Edgware Road, Marble Arch and Victoria. Routemasters had supplanted RT type vehicles on this and many other routes operating into central London once the trolleybus replacement programme was completed. Route 16 gained Routemasters in January 1963.

1998/87647

As congestion relentlessly increased through the 1960s, bus lanes began to appear as a practical way of managing the available road space, by giving buses priority over other traffic. The first bus lanes were introduced in 1968 on Vauxhall Bridge Road; this high profile southbound lane between Marble Arch and Hyde Park Corner is seen here at the bottom of Park Lane alongside the Hilton Hotel. Operating during the Monday to Friday evening peak periods, its implementation was helped by taking part of Hyde Park's eastern margin to increase the road width, allowing three lanes for other traffic to flow. In more confined streets such generous provision was not possible and one-way schemes also became a common way of managing traffic.

1998/44964

When it opened in 1968, as the first new Tube for 50 years, the Victoria line revolutionised travel from north and north-east London into the West End. Many bus routes had to be altered as travel patterns changed. During the line's construction major work was undertaken at Oxford Circus, where a new ticket hall was built under the busy road junction of Oxford Street and Regent Street. A temporary bridge-like structure known as the 'umbrella' was in place between August 1963 and Easter 1968, to carry traffic across the intersection, and allow construction to continue beneath.

1998/61970

Traffic congestion in Swiss Cottage at the beginning of the 1960s, with a bus of RT type struggling south on route 2 to Norwood Garage. In common with many trunk bus services at the time, the 2 ran right across London, connecting North Finchley, Golders Green and Crystal Palace. Although the practice of long-distance itineraries minimised the need for passengers to change buses, it meant such lengthy routes were bedeviled with unreliability caused by traffic congestion, and were progressively shortened.

1998/44791

Route 500 brought many innovations on its introduction in April 1966: the Red Arrow branding; high capacity single deck operation with the majority of passengers standing; coin in the slot turnstile entry; change-giving machines; centre exit doors; a route and timetable designed for commuters in the peak and shoppers in the off-peak. All of these features took some time to catch on but proved remarkably successful and have stood the test of time, except for the turnstile and cumbersome change machine. Indeed, the flat fare idea later spread across the bus network, thanks to new ticketing technology.

1998/43625

London's buses have always played a key role in high profile sporting events. The 'Derby' horse racing day at Epsom and lawn tennis at Wimbledon would see additional buses provided to take supporters from nearby stations to the venues. No record of events during the 1960s would be complete without reference to England's outstanding victory in the World Cup on 30 July 1966. Together, London Transport and British Rail produced bespoke publicity and maintained close operational working to ensure the massive crowds were moved efficiently.

1998/55126

To help alleviate the crippling staff shortage affecting London Transport in the early 1960s, recruitment personnel went to the Caribbean to encourage people to move to London for a new life as a bus conductor or driver, and in many other roles. Typical of those attracted was Oli Jackson who came from Jamaica in 1965. Working conditions in the 1960s were not good and Mr Jackson was motivated by his experiences to become a trade union activist in the T&GWU whilst working at Peckham bus garage. He later became an official in that union and represented bus workers' interests nationally.

1998/18624

Soon after route 500 commenced operation the report *Reshaping London's Bus Services* was published in September 1966 outlining the Board's radical plans to deal with worsening traffic congestion and staff shortages. Changing travel patterns also had to be accommodated: it was expected that there would be increased demand for peak (rush hour) travel compared to off-peak, and for shorter rather than longer distance journeys. The Plan outlined how routes would be curtailed, how one-person operation would be extended throughout the bus fleet, how more standing accommodation would be provided; and how new (mechanised) methods of fare collection would be pursued.

1998/108710

The driver seated in the cab is a driving instructor while another instructor from the Chiswick training school on the left talks to a trainee bus inspector. London Transport was a major employer of migrants from the Caribbean right through to the 1970s. Whilst staff were recruited directly to fill essential posts in the company, for some time many black employees did not progress to more senior roles. No official policy caused this, but discrimination often resulted in applications for promotion being rejected. The first black inspector was appointed in the late 1960s.

2005/17172

London Transport was a very hierarchical organisation, proud of the traditions, which dated back to its formation in 1933. By the late 1960s its well-established structure and roles, based on a cross between the Civil Service and the military, began to look outdated and inappropriate in a fast-changing society. This posed shot of a Country Bus inspector in the smart uniform of the time was taken in September 1969 just before the formation of London Country Bus Services Ltd. Gordon Petrie worked on the buses all his life and ended his career as Chief Inspector at High Wycombe and Amersham garages.

1998/87046

When London Transport first trialled double deck front entrance buses in 1965, it chose the Leyland Atlantean (XA) and Daimler Fleetline (XF). Not far behind, however, was its own home-made variant of the Routemaster, the FRM. Made from 60 per cent standard Routemaster parts, this bus appeared in 1966, and was used experimentally on a number of routes, including local service 284 in Potters Bar. With Routemasters still being introduced as late as 1968, FRM1 was too late to be adopted for production, as London Transport opted for buying standard buses from vehicle manufacturers rather than creating its own, bespoke but uneconomic, types.

2002/3822

The so-called bus of the 1970s was not destined to become an icon. Christened the 'Londoner', a title which never stuck, the Fleetline DMS class first served on route 95 (and 220) in 1971. It was one of the least successful bus types operated by London Transport.

2004/16203

Aside from the route changes and increased vehicle numbers
resulting from trolleybus replacement, and the introduction
of one-way streets, the bus network remained relatively
fixed during the first half of the 1960s. Large areas of housing
remained unserved, and Hampstead was one of the few
Underground stations not on the bus network. This gap was
filled in 1968 when route 268 began operating through narrow
Heath Street, providing a link to Swiss Cottage. The difficult
to manoeuvre MB type single deck bus was not popular with
some residents of Hampstead, who liked the idea that their
'village' was a bus free zone.

1998/44508

Before extension of the Piccadilly line in the mid-1970s, a fleet of specially adapted Routemasters carried both passengers and their luggage bus services from west London to the main airport at Heathrow. In summer 1969 the Airport Express service was inaugurated, to link Hounslow West station with Heathrow Central bus station and the three terminal buildings, and to create closer links with the innovation of jet-powered transportation. Air crews, passengers and airport workers paid a flat (single value) fare to use the MB type buses on route A1, which joined existing bus and Green Line coach services at this massive travel hub.

David Lawrence collection

LONDON TRANSPORT MAGAZINE

September 1969   Threepence

New express bus for London Airport

(REPORT AND PICTURES IN THIS ISSUE)

In preparation for decimalisation a trial fare system comprising the Haines fare collection box was installed on flat fare suburban routes, to replace the unpopular self-service ticket machines and turnstiles. Passengers dropped the exact fare into a transparent box and the driver would then operate a lever allowing the money to fall into a sealed container. No tickets were issued. Demonstrating the new fare collection system is Mrs Jacqueline Cutler, from the LT publicity office, shown here with bus driving instructor David Morgan at Chiswick Works.

2004/16200

PAY HERE

9ᴰ ADULT

6ᴰ CHILD

Few additional roads gained buses during the 1960s, as lines of route remained much as they had for some decades, perhaps necessitating a long walk to the bus stop. This changed in September 1972 when the first of four new minibus routes began operating on previously unserved roads. Seen here in the grounds of Highlands Hospital (since converted to a residential estate), is an FS class Ford minibus on route W9 which ran between Enfield and Southgate via Grange Park and Winchmore Hill with a 10p flat fare. The W9 grew in popularity as travellers appreciated the convenience of having a bus close to their home. Of interest too is the white 'roundel' symbol on the vehicle side: this was the product of London Transport's revision of its corporate identity, or brand, from 1972.
1998/68414

Three Routemaster buses head west along the newly-opened bus lane in Piccadilly in May 1973. This arrangement proved controversial due to its contra-flow nature. While it saved considerable additional mileage and journey time, and provided more convenient bus stops in Piccadilly itself, pedestrians became confused and some nasty accidents took place. The buses shown are on routes 38, 14 and 9 and the Royal Academy can be seen with rows of Union Jack flags outside.
1998/84508

The success of the first minibus routes led the GLC to ask London Transport to consider buses for unserved roads in Hampstead Garden Suburb. Taking into account the affluence of this area, and the desire to test the demand for a more personal bus service, the operation was introduced on a dial-a-bus basis with no fixed route. Passengers telephoned a central control point based in Golders Green bus station which arranged a pick-up and set-down as near as possible to their front doors. This operation continues in part today as the H2.
1998/66052

The vehicle challenges faced by London Transport in the 1970s lurched from one crisis to another. After the disastrous Fleetline DMS class had been delivered, a batch of MCW bodied Scanias named the 'Metropolitan' were purchased. In use from 1976, these also proved difficult for engineers to keep on the road, hampered further by the country's economic and industrial problems leading to shortages of spare parts. That some of these vehicles lasted for just four years, and all 164 had been withdrawn by 1983, may reflect more on the lack of appropriate skills among the engineering staff than on the vehicles themselves.

1998/60664

NEW TYPE BUSES
on Route 50
STARTING JULY 24

London's bus services are being converted to one-man operation. One-man buses save staff and higher 'one-man' wages will help recruiting. More economical operating may save some routes from being withdrawn or severely reduced.

From the mid-1970s some Daimler Fleetline OPO buses were introduced to trunk routes with conductors as for a time London Transport slackened its programme of route conversions, it was recognised that without improved fare collection technology busy trunk services, such as the 149 seen here passing the Bank of England, needed to retain a full crew. During this period front entrance bus doors were painted bright yellow to help passengers see the boarding point.

2002/19008

Queen Elizabeth II succeeded to the throne in 1952 and her Silver Jubilee was marked throughout June 1977. Celebrations in London included a royal procession down the Mall. Here two Routemaster buses are passing through the gates of Buckingham Palace during the event. The normally red buses had been painted silver especially for the occasion. Twenty-five buses were treated in this way (and renumbered SRM 1 to SRM 25); the advertising rights were sold to sponsors including Tate and Lyle (RM 1902) and Farley's Rusks (RM 1907) for £10,000 each.

2005/18979

London Transport never missed the opportunity to celebrate a special occasion, and the 150th anniversary of George Shillibeer's Omnibus service was marked in 1979 by twelve RMs and a Daimler DMS wearing a very attractive livery based on Shillibeer's original, as depicted here on RM2186.

1998/65233

Photographed in 1978 is the body of RM2148 suspended in Aldenham Works, Elstree, Hertfordshire, as it undergoes an overhaul. Bodies were detached from the chassis and moved by crane from the dismount area (where the front and rear sub-frames were removed) to the High Bay where repairs were undertaken. By the late 1970s the Routemaster had been due to be replaced, but with the continuing difficulties presented by off-the-peg rear engine buses, the decision was made to keep more Routemasters and completely refurbish the remaining fleet.

2002/18948

A major cultural milestone was passed
in 1974 when Jill Viner passed her Public
Service Vehicle driving test, to become
London's first female bus driver. She
went on to drive from Norbiton garage
and worked there until it closed in 1993.
It was a huge psychological change
for women to be seen driving a bus in
the capital, although they had been
employed as 'clippies' (conductresses)
on a permanent basis since the end of
the Second World War.

1998/83575

After the Conservatives took control of the GLC in 1977 investment in London Transport suffered. By the end of the decade, when this photograph of Mill Hill East Underground station was taken, parts of the infrastructure were looking distinctly unattractive and shabby. There is the option of a ramp to the station entrance for those with disabilities, but the buses and trains would have been inaccessible, and although the network map displayed in the shelter is a helpful addition, the rudimentary nature of the shelter itself – offering minimal protection for waiting passengers – definitely belonged to a past generation.

2001/16531

The pace of cultural change once women became bus drivers can be appreciated by this photograph taken in 1976, just two years after Jill Viner's achievement. A black female inspector is supervising another female bus driver. Just a few years earlier such a scene would have been unthinkable, with many male employees, and the trade unions, deeply suspicious of giving increased responsibilities to women.

2005/15317

Behind the scenes, London Transport employed hundreds of support staff who kept the large complex system moving. These included catering staff working at the organisation's Food Production Centre in Croydon. Staff prepared food to be sent out to staff canteens across London. One woman is operating the mincing machine and two are sorting the newly made sausages in this picture taken some time in the late 1970s. When the centre opened in 1950, it had the capacity to produce 5,000 pounds (nearly 2,300 kilograms) of sausages per week.

2002/18110

Perhaps the most memorable transport image of the 1970s was the Concorde supersonic jet plane, which made its first commercial flight from London Heathrow to New York in May 1976. Here it flies over Hatton Cross station, from which connecting buses operated to the central airport area until the Piccadilly line was extended to Terminals 1, 2 and 3 in 1977. Seen here in front of the station is a DMS on route 90B, which at that time ran from Kew Gardens to Yeading and Northolt without serving the airport itself.

2006/363

In the 1970s the market for sightseeing bus tours around central London was not yet exploited to the extent that it is now. On behalf of London Transport, contractors operated tours with a range of buses which had been drawn from other fleets. They included the open-top format as seen here at the tour's Piccadilly Circus boarding point in July 1972.

1998/57284

London Transport also ran a programme of excursions to landmarks at London's edges, including Windsor and its Castle. This Tour Guide is addressing a group of tourists outside St George's Chapel in 1978. Typically for the time the guide is wearing a traditional London Transport uniform complete with 'bullseye' cap badge, which contrasts with the more casual attire favoured today.

1998/44353

In addition to bespoke tours targeted at tourists, London Transport continued its tradition of using poster designs to encourage more use of the standard network of bus routes. This recognised the greater leisure time available to many people as the working week contracted to five days, leaving a full weekend for recreation. This poster was designed by Hans Unger and Eberhard Schulze in 1970 and promotes travel by bus to historic sites and leisure attractions across London. Unger and Schulze used white marble blocks to make the mosaic: both the original model and the completed poster are in the collection of the London Transport Museum.

1980/113

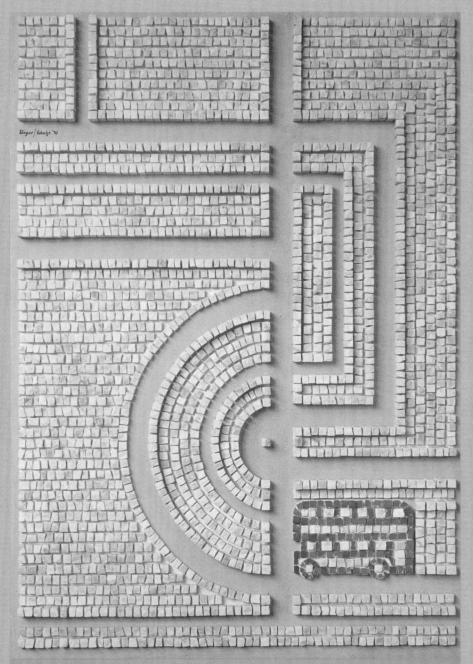

BUSABOUT The London red bus, its top deck high above the traffic, is your ideal grandstand view-point, for historic buildings, places of interest and the endlessly entertaining hubbub of the teeming streets. A Red Bus Rover ticket gives you a day's travel-as-you-please on 1,500 miles of red bus routes and costs 7/– (child 3/6). A leaflet gives details. Another leaflet 'London from a Bus Top' suggests a lot of ways to use it. Ask at any London Transport Travel Enquiry office or write to the Public Relations Officer, 55 Broadway, S.W.1.

BY LONDON TRANSPORT ⊖

Printed in England by Sir Joseph Causton and Sons Ltd, London and Eastleigh

UNDERGROUND

FARE STAGE

BUS STOP

W 9 MON TO SAT
MUSWELL HILL
BROADWAY

W 9 MUSWELL HILL, Broadway
Via Highlands Hospital
Southgate

EASTERN NATIONAL

ED 1052   TJN 975W

LONDON
REGIONAL
TRANSPORT
SERVICE

13

Fares Fair to privatisation, 1980–99

Roger Torode

The 1980s and 1990s brought the greatest change to London's buses since the creation of London Transport in 1933. The first stage had come in 1979 when operations were reorganised into eight Bus Districts. Two of these were in central London, while outer London was divided into six segments. District General Managers were introduced to take responsibility for the performance of buses in their area and to provide a local focus for service provision and marketing. At the same time, the Conservative government of the 1980s pushed forward a programme of deregulation, competitive tendering and privatisation throughout the public sector, whilst the Labour-led Greater London Council (GLC) elected in 1981 began giving financial support to improve the services on bus and Underground and to reduce fares – the 'Fares Fair' scheme. A legal challenge by the London Borough of Bromley eventually went to the House of Lords, who ruled the GLC fare reductions unlawful. A revised fares scheme was successfully introduced, but the relationship between the Conservative government and the Labour GLC was so bad on this and other issues that it moved to disband the GLC, transferring their powers to itself and the London Boroughs.

The London Regional Transport Act of 1983 created a new organisation, responsible to the Secretary of State for Transport, who took control from June 1984 – the only case of nationalisation by that Government. London Regional Transport (LRT) was to be a small holding company with bus and Underground operations established as separate subsidiaries.

One of the major provisions of the Act was that LRT should 'provide or secure the provision of services', rather than necessarily provide them itself, and it obliged LRT to 'invite the submission of tenders for certain activities where it is thought appropriate'. The new organisation was keen to introduce competition into its services whilst maintaining a single comprehensive network. It therefore began tendering the operation of individual bus routes, or groups of routes, to private bus companies. Some of these already ran services in the areas around London, while others had previous experience in coaching, contract work and private hire, but were new to bus operations. So although buses outside London were deregulated from 1986, leading to competition on the road, those in London continued to be planned and coordinated by LRT with competition for the contract to run the service – competition *for* the road, rather than *on* the road.

The first routes were advertised in 1984, and new operators commenced in 1985. Over the initial two years of tendering, 205 bids were submitted for 55 tenders and cost reductions averaging 20 per cent were delivered on those routes. By the end of 1986, 13.5 million miles of bus service had been tendered – approaching one eighth of LT's total bus mileage, a considerable achievement in just two years of tendering. Just under half the routes (45 per cent) were won by London Buses Ltd (LBL), a part of LRT, 40 per cent by subsidiaries of the National Bus Company and 15 per cent by independent operators. Vehicle mileage went up, reliability improved, and revenue increased.

In order to compete more effectively, London Buses created a number of low-cost operations in place of existing garages, some of which were closed. The 1983 Act also allowed other bus operators to run services with the agreement of the Traffic

VEHICLE MILEAGE WENT UP, RELIABILITY IMPROVED, AND REVENUE INCREASED

Commissioners, rather than requiring the approval of London Regional Transport. However, a proposal by AMOS (Associated Minibus Operators Ltd) to run high frequency minibus services on four trunk routes across central London using 500 vehicles was turned down by both LRT and by the Minister of Transport, because it could be a chaotic addition to the pressure on London's streets. Nevertheless, a number of minibus schemes were introduced throughout London to improve the penetration of buses into residential areas that had not previously had a service. In other cases, traditional buses with conductors were replaced on some routes by minibuses which, though smaller, provided a more frequent service of one-person operated buses at a similar cost. The better service also attracted more passengers with very good results.

Tendering of routes and continuous cost cutting saw revenue support to LRT halved between 1984 and 1988. This helped bolster the case for LRT to continue planning and tendering the bus network. Government policy was for both privatisation and deregulation, but whilst the bus companies were privatised in 1994, deregulation was not in the end brought to London due to concerns over the chaos that had resulted in other major cities. In these, different bus operators competed for passengers on the street and responsibility for unremunerative evening and weekend services passed to the local authorities to let by competitive tender. The wish to keep a coordinated bus network linked to the Underground, to exploit the proven benefits of the Travelcard, and to avoid open competition (as had occurred with the 'pirate' buses in the 1920s), eventually led to this change which was solely in London. The government still intended to privatise London's bus operations however. In preparation for this process and to improve local management and accountability, LBL created 11 bus operating units which would compete with each other, and with other operators.

Formed at the end of 1988, these companies became wholly-owned limited companies in 1989. They had to significantly reduce their operating costs, and so worked to change the pay and conditions packages of bus crews in order to be able to compete with other operators – otherwise they would lose all of the work to those operators, whose pay rates would then prevail. London bus crews were proud of their conditions of service, which had been built up over many years, and they were unwilling to lose them. Industrial action resulted in many areas of London and in one case led to that subsidiary, London Forest, losing an entire garage of work and being closed - its remaining work was distributed to other LBL companies. Nevertheless, all the companies introduced comparable pay rates in the following years.

LONDON TRANSPORT'S BUS COMPANIES WERE PRIVATISED IN 1994

The bus operating companies were all sold into the private sector in 1994 and early 1995. Four of these were management buyouts with staff involvement, whilst six were sold to existing UK bus groups to extend their operations into London. The management buyout companies were all sold on to other groups in the following years, and some are now owned by multi-national transport businesses. This brought to an end over 60 years of direct bus operations by London Transport, and all London's buses were now running under contract to LRT.

Routemasters crossing Westminster Bridge in June 1984. In the background is County Hall, the headquarters of the Greater London Council, with a roof banner directed at the Houses of Parliament reading 'Peers, Listen to Londoners, Don't scrap the GLC elections'. The right- hand bus has adverts reading 'Keep GLC Working for London'. London Transport was taken over by the government on 29 June 1984 and the GLC was closed down in 1986.

Roger Torode

Keeping the service running in all
weathers, a Leyland Titan braves
the snow in January 1982 near
Walthamstow garage. The Titan was
a new generation of double-decker,
designed for one-person operation on
intensive city services, and including
lessons learned from the Routemaster.
Between 1978 and 1984, 1,125 Titans
entered service, together with 1,442
Metrobuses from MCW.

Roger Torode

One-person operation (OPO) of services
gradually extended throughout London,
and the Routemaster became a rare
sight in the suburbs. Long route 69 from
North Woolwich through Canning Town,
Stratford, Leyton and Walthamstow to
Chingford kept its Routemasters until
February 1985, and one is seen here
in 1984 climbing Chingford Mount. In
the past, this service saw heavy use in
holiday periods carrying east-enders
to Chingford Plains and the Royal
Forest Hotel.

Roger Torode

In 1981, long before privatisation, one of the private sector's Sightseeing Tour buses was hired by the ruling Labour group at the GLC to campaign for the 'Fares Fair' scheme, and against the ruling by the Law Lords which ended it. A modified scheme was introduced a few months later. From left to right on the top deck are: Tony Banks MP, Andy Harris GLC councillor, Ken Livingstone Labour leader of the GLC and Valerie Wise Deputy Leader. The bus had previously been used on the Round London Sightseeing Tour. Dave Wetzel, the GLC's Transport Committee chair, was the unsuspecting driver of this red bus unaware it was not owned by London Transport.

LT News

A longstanding tradition amongst London busmen was to take an excursion to the seaside on a summer Sunday for staff and their families. The garage Sports and Social Club would organise the hire using a volunteer driver. Routemasters from Streatham and Catford garage are seen here at Brighton in August 1980.

Roger Torode

Passenger boarding on OPO buses was too slow for central London services, so Routemasters with conductors were retained for some years. At busy suburban centres, passengers would arrive at the bus stop more quickly than they could board the vehicle, and long queues developed. At the Victoria line's Walthamstow terminus, passengers press forward to board a 212 in 1982.

Roger Torode

Ogle Design of Letchworth carried out a major research project for London Buses to improve the design and layout of OPO double decker vehicles for drivers and passengers. This rig was created to test alternative entrance layouts and step arrangements, using members of the public to act as 'passengers' in the tests. The result was a revised design for the interior layout of the bus, two-stream boarding with an angled entrance and an additional exit step which together improved the accessibility, speed of boarding and alighting.

Ogle Design

A new ticketing system named 'Autocheck' was developed as part of the Ogle research, using readers that could check the magnetic cards then in use on the Underground, and so allow two-stream boarding on buses. These devices worked through the new electronic drivers' ticket machines which were then replacing mechanical equipment. This picture shows 'passengers' evaluating the equipment at London Transport's Chiswick Works before the public trial. Autocheck started in March 1987 but proved problematic as the card readers were precision equipment which suffered from the constant vibrations of a bus travelling over London's roads, and from dust, oil and water entering the machine. Additionally card-based tickets would expand in wet weather and cause the reader to jam.

Roger Torode

Red Arrow services provided fast connections between the main line stations in central London, operating with a flat fare dropped into a box to speed-up boarding. The routes were upgraded in 1981 with Leyland National II single-deckers. This example is passing the Mansion House on route 501 to London Bridge Station.

2001/56659

The Ogle design features were incorporated into the Leyland Olympian double-deckers delivered in 1986/7. Many of these were used in the Thamesmead area for the public trial of Autocheck magnetic ticketing, alongside older buses.

2002/578

The Round London Sightseeing Tour was developed in 1986 with Routemasters converted to open top form. The service was facing significant competition in the growing tourist market. and was enhanced and branded the 'Official' tour to counter rivals. RM752 is seen in Trafalgar Square.

David Cole

Routemasters continued to provide mainstream central London services and had become an icon of London. In 1981 a fleet of decorated buses was launched to celebrate the Royal Wedding of Prince Charles and Lady Diana Spencer in July. Commercial advertisers sponsored the vehicles to promote their products.

1998/65282

There had been all-night public transport in London for decades. Night bus services were extensively developed in the early 1980s to provide for the city's growing nightlife. Routes had previously been focused on Fleet Street for the print workers, but were reshaped to provide hourly services, with interchange based on Trafalgar Square, chosen as it could handle the crowds that built up rapidly as clubs and bars emptied.

2005/869

The first services to be tendered for private operation were advertised in 1984 and the first contracts commenced in July 1985. Route W9 from Enfield to Muswell Hill passed to Eastern National, whose single-decker with LT symbols is seen at Southgate Station. Passengers were surprised to find green buses with coach seats on their local route, and 'London Transport Service' signs were displayed to reassure them that this was their bus!

Mike Harris

Routes crossing the Greater London boundary into the Home Counties were also tendered early in the programme. This was done jointly with the County Councils who were required to competitively tender all subsidised services, and because of the greater likelihood of finding willing operators on the fringes of London. This London Country Leyland Atlantean is working route 403 to West Croydon, the red LRT sign helpfully letting everyone know its function.

John Parkin

The development of purpose built midibuses, made by manufacturers including Optare of Leeds, was a breakthrough, giving 25 seats and much greater comfort. Their size transformed the economics of running small buses. This Optare CityPacer is seen at Orpington on R3 to Petts Wood. Similar vehicles commenced a central London midibus route C1 in October 1986 linking Parliament Square, Victoria, Sloane Square and Kensington.

2002/854

Crews at Ash Grove Garage mark the end of their operation of route 22 in 1990. The western segment of the route was subsequently operated from Putney Garage, while the eastern portion was converted to OPO and run by Kentish Bus following tendering. Ash Grove had provided Routemasters on the 22 until 1987, and OPO buses on Sundays from that time. Ash Grove staff ran a special Routemaster on their last day, driven by Derek Bull and Alan Rice (on the left) and conducted by Keith Hunte (on the right). Keith Hunte had regularly worked the route since becoming a London bus conductor in 1961.

Roger Torode collection

A 1983 report by the Monopolies and Mergers Commission on London Regional Transport's Chiswick and Aldenham vehicle works concluded that they were unable to be competitive. Aldenham was not designed to cope with the new generation of buses - whose chassis could not be removed from the bodies for overhaul - and new regulations required an annual test for buses which was better prepared for in the garages. Bus maintenance was gradually transferred to the indivdual garages and the works were sold. Driver training was also transferred to the local Districts in 1986 and the Chiswick Driving School, including its famous skid pan, was closed.

2014/5291

With much publicity, the first central London service to be tendered was the 24, a famous route from Hampstead Heath to Pimlico via Trafalgar Square, Westminster and Victoria. In November 1988 the 24 passed to Grey-Green Coaches of Stamford Hill, who bought a new fleet of Volvo buses in an attractive grey, green and orange livery. Grey-Green was a long-standing coach operator with roots back to the horse carriage business set up by George Ewer in 1885. Their traditional work of taking north and east Londoners to the seaside in Kent and East Anglia was declining as Londoners moved to the suburbs and bought cars, and Grey-Green gradually moved their interests to London bus operations.

2014/5359

In a bold move, the London Buses subsidiary CentreWest converted two busy central London Routemaster services to high-frequency midibus operation in Spring 1989. This was very controversial, with some passengers objecting to the new vehicles, but CentreWest demonstrated an impressive increase in passengers at no overall increase in cost, having replaced big buses with a crew of two with smaller driver-only vehicles.

Barry Le Jeune

The first Routemaster service to be tendered was the 19, a high-profile route from Battersea Bridge to Finsbury Park via King's Road, Chelsea, Hyde Park Corner, Piccadilly Circus, Shaftesbury Avenue, Holborn and the Angel Islington. This was contracted to Kentish Bus from April 1993, who, for a fresh start, recruited conductors with sales experience rather than bus experience. The vehicles were owned by LRT and painted in Kentish Bus colours. Here a 19 is followed by a red London General 14 through Cambridge Circus.

Keith Wood

London United introduced a number of midibus schemes with local branding, rather than the 'hoppa' name used elsewhere in London. The Harrier network around Richmond was launched alongside a Harrier jet aircraft – which might be faster but carried fewer passengers - the name selected to emphasise the agile nature of the new buses. London United claimed an 11 per cent increase in passengers on routes where these vehicles replaced double-deckers.

Martin Whitley

The London bus network is complex and can be difficult to understand, particularly for visitors. Improved marketing of routes suitable for tourists - such as the 15 seen here at the Tower of London - was developed in the 1980s. This bus has additional publicity specific to its route, while the bus stop is also labelled with clear information. Interestingly, the bus stop flag is from a previous era, divided vertically to show that both red buses and Green Line coaches stop there.

2014/5283

Minibus schemes opened up bus driving jobs to a far larger group of the population, as shown by the young woman here driving an Eastern National W11 at Walthamstow Central. As bus design improved, with automatic transmissions and power steering, many women found they could move onto full size vehicles. Operators responded by reviewing their recruitment practices: whilst in the past they selected staff able to drive heavy vehicles and taught them customer service, now they would look for staff with customer service experience and train them to drive buses.

Colin Stannard

In 1990 a new service was developed by LRT and the London Docklands Development Corporation (LDDC) to connect the burgeoning new Docklands financial zone with Waterloo Station, which was to be the terminus for cross-channel international railway links. London Forest won the new route by competitive tender, and designed a special livery with the LDDC. The service was launched by Michael Portillo, then the Minister of State for Transport, who is seen driving through the ceremonial tape.

Roger Torode

Route 159 traditionally ran from West Hampstead to South Croydon, and even further on Sundays. Like other routes it was shortened to improve reliability and to allow one-person operation (OPO) of the outer sections. In 1992, when the 159 ran from Baker St to Streatham, South London introduced this attractive colour scheme based on a heritage Brighton bus livery. In 1999 the route was again shortened to run from Marble Arch, and in 2005 it was famously the last regular service to be run by Routemasters, being converted to OPO in December that year.

Colin Fradd

In November 1993 buses from all 19 independent operators running LRT tendered services were photographed at North Weald airdrome to show the range of companies, vehicles and liveries then involved in London bus tendering. These were in addition to the London Buses companies which were about to be privatised.

2014/5340

A new off-bus ticketing experiment commenced in 1992, using contactless smartcards. The first equipment for this application came from Finland, where it was used for ski-lift passes. A small trial was conducted from September 1992 on route 212, chosen because it used just five dedicated vehicles with regular staff and passengers. The cards had only to be touched against the cardreader, rather than inserted, and the solid state technology was expected to be reliable in the on-bus environment. This trial was successful with regular passengers using the cards on buses in full service. Following the initial smartcard project, the Harrow area was chosen for a larger scale trial, albeit still relatively self-contained in terms of buses, passengers and staff. The programme started in February 1994 on 200 buses, and 20,000 contactless smartcards were issued to staff and holders of Freedom Passes, Travelcards and Bus Passes. The system worked well, speeding up boarding and removing the need for detailed checking of passes by the driver.

Roger Torode collection

Get smart with

SMARTCARD

Here's your chance to help London Transport test an exciting new ticket technology.

Route 212 has been specifically chosen as a test route for London Transport's new **Smartcard**.

Smartcard is an electronic revolution in fare collection and we need passengers like you to help us research this new system.

Smartcard is a contactless card which is read by a special machine or reader when you board the bus.

The benefits of the Smartcard system are:-

- Fast bus boarding times
- Easy to use
- High security level
- Very reliable technology

If you would like to take part in this test project which will last until Christmas 1992, please fill in the application form overleaf. Alternatively, you can write to us:
The SVT Project Team, London Transport, FREEPOST, London, SW1 0YH,
or phone us on:

071 918 4123

London Transport Service

Your help now will make bus travel better.

CentreWest's Gold Arrow services continued to grow passenger numbers and soon needed larger buses. This Dennis Dart, seen in 1995 on route 70, was bodied by Wright's of Ballymena, County Antrim who themselves developed from building small buses to double-deckers, and are now the manufacturer of the New Routemaster.
2003/3273

The final stage of the smartcard trial in February 1995, introduced the Harrow Bus Farecard, on which passengers could place a monetary credit which was deducted as journeys were made. The system also automatically capped their spending each day at the price of a local Bus Pass. The card was launched by Norman Cohen, Operating Services Director of LT Buses, with the Mayor of Harrow. Together with parallel work on London Underground, this led directly to the Oyster card of today.

Roger Torode

The London Buses subsidiary companies were all privatised in 1994 and January 1995. Four companies were sold to their management teams with staff involvement, and six were sold to existing UK bus groups. The sale, which raised £233 million, was launched at Hyde Park Corner on 24 March 1994 by Steven Norris, Minister for Transport in London (right) and Clive Hodson, Managing Director of London Buses (left).

London Transport Museum

Low floor buses were a significant development of the 1990s. They were found to help all passengers, not just the disabled, but also those with pushchairs or luggage. The first models appeared in 1994, and by 1998 all new single-deckers were low floor accessible models. Development then moved to double-deckers. This Dennis Dart also 'kneels' at stops by expelling air from the front suspension, which is then replenished before the bus moves off.
2003/3931

Countdown indicators were a popular innovation, giving real time arrival data for the next bus on each route. The system was costly, and focussed on busy stops where large numbers of passengers would benefit. Paradoxically, these stops had a more frequent service and so less need for the information! Now, in 2014, smartphone applications are a more cost-effective way of communicating bus movements to travellers.

2003/3265

14

New Routemaster: the bus bounces back, 2000–2014

Leon Daniels

The return of local government to London in 2000, with the creation of the Greater London Authority (GLA), heralded a renaissance in bus travel. Elected as first Mayor of London was the opinionated Ken Livingstone whose tenure as Leader (1981-86) of the Greater London Council had been abruptly cut short when Margaret Thatcher abolished it. Livingstone made Transport for London (TfL), the new organisation responsible for administering travel networks in the metropolis, very accountable and transparent. He pushed through cheaper fares, free travel for the young and the old, and allowed a revolution that produced the congestion charge, considerable increases in bus volumes, and bigger vehicles to deliver them.

New governments can be radical and here there was a radical leader as well. Ken Livingstone believed that the bus was the life blood for Londoners - to get to work and to look for it, to travel to school, for leisure and as a serious alternative to the private car. His Congestion Charge attracted many critics, some noting that in the Mayoral election the arch capitalist Steven Norris opposed charging for the scarce resource of street space, whilst his heavily left-leaning rival Livingstone promoted it. The electorate took this contradiction in its stride but many were surprised when Livingstone delivered on his promise. Having shaved the top slice off London's traffic volumes, and delivered greater capacity buses, Livingstone had established a virtuous circle. Demographically, London's upper middle, middle and lower middle social groups (the ABC1s) transferred to the buses, releasing road space previously occupied by private motor transport. More benefits followed. Not only did Ken Livingstone give superior free travel to the over 60s - allowing them to also travel in the morning peak hours - he gave it to the young as well. Children under 18 could now travel free on buses. Astutely the Mayor knew these concessions could never be reversed.

Growing passenger numbers demanded bigger vehicles, and TfL was already working at top speed to deliver a fully-accessible bus fleet, years before the mandatory deadline set out in legislation. The continental articulated bus, already in service in several UK cities, was deployed. Over 300 vehicles - a lengthened version of the Mercedes Benz Citaro - would follow into London service, their 135-passenger capacity, and ease of entry/exit welcomed. They ran on the main arterial roads and on the Central London Red Arrow services. Some other Central London and busy trunk routes were also converted to articulated bus operation. Open boarding was a new phenomenon: doors at the front, middle and rear could be used to board or alight. Some worsening in fare collection was inevitable, notwithstanding such a high level of Oyster smartcard adoption. The level of fare evasion became a target for the popular press, as did ill-informed criticism about their contribution to congestion. Eventually a 'cause celebre' was established and, incredibly, the 2008 Mayoral election started to turn on the suitability, or otherwise, of the tabloid-christened 'Bendy Bus'.

The New Mayor in City Hall was Boris Johnson, who had included in his manifesto the promise that London's articulated buses would be 'dispatched to some Scandinavian airport' when he gained office. Considering TfL, Boris Johnson made some critical decisions. He retained Peter Hendy as Commissioner of Transport, and Tim O'Toole as Managing Director, London Underground, while promising to attack alleged spending excesses; in the event few were found. The headline news 'Bendy Bus' was, however, removed as promised, and the last of them ran in London Buses' service in December 2011. In truth their replacement by more conventional means of transportation incurred more cost - more drivers, more vehicles and compensation for the premature retirement of vehicles - but before the sun set on the articulated Citaro, Boris was back with a plan to give London a new iconic bus.

LONDON'S MIDDLE CLASSES TRANSFERRED TO THE BUSES

At the competition launch, designers and manufacturers were encouraged to come forward with radical proposals. Many of the entries were just that, and ultimately vehicle builders Wrightbus of Ballymena were paired with designer Thomas Heatherwick. The outcome, a stunning new design which has more than a nod to the DNA heritage of the past - the rear staircase of an NS type, the warmth of the Routemaster, the fast boarding of the articulated buses and the opportunity to recreate the chirpy London bus conductor riding on the rear platform. One important technological innovation was also present: these buses run on electricity for much of their journeys. The 'New Bus for London' turned out to be another item which followed the persona of the Mayor. Most loved it; a few hated it. In a period of severe economic restraint, the cost of conductors or 'Customer Assistants' was found to be less affordable than expected, whilst the brave attempt to eliminate opening windows on the vehicles allowed Mayoral critics to venture that they were 'saunas' when the weather outside was warm. In fact temperatures inside are about the same as ordinary buses. But the New Routemaster (a name given by users) was quickly appreciated. There were clamours for more of them in more places, and it became perfectly possible for them to run in driver-only mode very successfully. Passengers loved to travel on them: when they were introduced on a route also operated for heritage purposes with 'old' Routemasters, the latter quickly became less popular. The conductors/Customer Assistants - where provided - admitted that much of their time was taken up with photography…

On board, and in the streets, the electronic revolution was quietly taking place. In December 2012 contactless payment using credit and debit cards was introduced on buses. The take up was so good that by summer 2014 it was possible to eliminate cash fares on buses altogether. The media and critics warned that the end of civilisation was approaching: in reality it was introduced with hardly a ripple. Examination of consultation responses showed that most objections were on behalf of others: it seems that soon the 'others' were satisfied too. Another social change came with information provision. Some 2,500 bus stops were provided with real time Countdown information giving the expected arrivals of the next buses. Customers everywhere wanted more, but in a curious paradox the best business cases for additional information display were at busy stops where there actually lots of buses, whilst the need for information was greater in quieter places where the installation costs were hard to justify. Swooping in came the inevitable smartphone app. With Transport for London making real-time bus data freely available, entrepreneurs soon made it possible to deliver this information into the palm of the traveller's hand. No longer did the timid demand a policeman at every stop late at night: the smartphone app told you when to step outside and catch the bus.

So in 2014, London's bus passenger is electronically-capable, richly supplied with helpful information, and carried on the country's youngest and most accessible bus fleet, 24 hours a day. A far cry from George Shillibeer's modest start some 185 years ago.

'Thank you Routemaster…' poster by Suzanne Davies, 2005.
2005/19669

Arup Associates designed a streamlined metallic covered bus
station for the traffic island at Vauxhall Cross, creating a refuge
for the thousands of south Londoners interchanging here every
day between rail, road and Underground systems. Opened in
spring 2005, the bus station includes an information office
and real-time notifications of arrivals, for busy routes running
to the inner suburbs and the west end. The building may be
removed as part of redevelopment plans for 'Vauxhall Square',
and changes to traffic arrangements in the wider area.

TfL Media Library

Celebrations for Year of the Bus reached a literally show-
stopping peak with the Cavalcade of 22 June 2014. London's
major shopping thoroughfare Regent Street became a free
display of heritage and contemporary London buses, coordinated by the London Transport Museum and Transport for
London, with the Crown Estate and Regent Street Association.
TfL Press Office

To free-up land for the London 2012 Olympic site in east London, a new bus garage was developed in Canning Town, and named West Ham. Planned to be environmentally sensitive - it has a wind turbine to meet some of its electricity needs - the garage was designed by Pringle Richards Sharratt Architects with engineers Arup, and is capable of accommodating 320 buses including lower-emission electro-diesel hybrid vehicles. It was completed in 2010.

TfL Media Library

A bus driver configures the on-board iBus communications system, 2013.

TfL Media Library

CentreComm is the emergency command and control centre for London Buses. First established in 1979, it operates round-the-clock and it in constant contact with some 8,500 buses using GPS and the iBus radio system. Here an operator views a vehicle's details during a call, 2014.

TfL Media Library

London's last Routemaster buses ran in scheduled passenger carrying service in December 2005. RM875 heads south along Brixton Hill towards Streatham, on route 159. In 2014, Transport for London still operates Routemaster buses on route 15 between Trafalgar Square and the Tower of London.

2006/1632

Close up of the bus display on a prototype digital bus stop at Piccadilly Circus, 2014.

TfL Media Library

The special silver bus LT150, created for the Year of the Bus celebrations, and parked outside City Hall in January 2014.

TfL Media Library

NOTES

Introduction

[1] The Reinohl Collection was originally put together as a collection of tickets by two brothers. Herbert J Reinohl started collecting tickets as a youth in 1894. A few years later he was joined in his hobby by his younger brother, Albert F Reinohl. After the First World War, in addition to tickets, they began to take an interest in the study of all London omnibus and tramway routes from the time of the introduction of the first omnibus in 1829. As a result they extracted records of routes from London guides in the British Museum and gathered material from every available source, so as to record all this information in their collection. Herbert Reinohl travelled extensively with the British Forces and in addition to provincial material, he sent back items from overseas, for his brother to add to the collection. The brothers presented the collection to the Institute of Transport by Deed of Gift in October 1936 and the Institute deciding it was more appropriate, eventually passed it to the London Transport Museum.

[2] Metropolitan Cammell-Weymann motor bodies from 1932, based at Addlestone, Surrey.

[3] Based in Park Royal, west London.

[4] Albert Athur Molteno Durrant was born in 1899. He joined the LGOC in 1919 as technical assistant to the engineer of the company, and in 1920 became experimental and research engineer. He began working for London Transport in 1935. During the Second World War he was appointed to the post of Director of Tank Design in the armoured fighting vehicle division of the Ministry of Supply. His team were responsible for improving the design of the Cromwell tank and for the design of the Centurion tank. This later became the basis for the Chieftain, the main battle tank for the British Army. He was made CBE in 1945. Durrant is regarded by many as the father of the highly successful RT and Routemaster families of buses. As chief mechanical engineer (road services) he was responsible for the policy of fleet standardisation and interchangeability of parts which enabled Chiswick and Aldenham works to be developed on flow-line systems. He retired on 3 July 1965.

[5] See for example Barry Arnold & Mike Harris. *Reshaping London's Buses*. Harrow Weald: Capital Transport Publishing, 1982.

[6] In 1911 and 1934 these events were known as the 'British Empire Games'.

[7] This vehicle was reportedly RT4790, heavily altered for the programme to resemble an open top bus. See: www.thedoubledeckers.com/bus.htm [accessed 24 April 2014]

[8] The two films with red buses were *On the Buses* (1971) and *Mutiny on the Buses* (1972). These were not London but Southend, Essex, vehicles, and not of a design commonly used in London. They were, however, sufficiently recognisable as urban transportation to underpin the storylines.

[9] Heritage route 9 ceased operation in summer 2014. See leondaniels.blogspot.co.uk/2014/01/all-good-things-as-they-say-come-to-end.html. [accessed 24 April 2014]

[10] Supported by the Heritage Lottery Fund (grant of £750,000) and London Transport Museum Friends (£125,000).

Chapter 1: The horse bus, 1829–1914

[1] Minutes of the Police Committee of the Court of Aldermen, 31 January 1834.

[2] Latchford, A L, and H Pollins. *London General: the story of the London bus 1856–1956*. London: London Transport, 1956, p.16.

[3] Service information extracted from a list published in the summer of 1895 by the Statistical Department of the London County Council, re-arranged and tabulated by J C Gillham in April 1953.

[4] Drawing of Adams's Equirotal Omnibus in H C Moore *Omnibuses and cabs: their origin and history*, Chapman & Hall, 1902, p61. The omnibus was also praised in the letters page of *The Mechanics Magazine*, April 6th – September 28th, Vol XXXI, 1839, p. 37.

[5] By 1860 the LGOC was carrying over 40 million passengers – 'see: T C Barker and Michael Robbins', *A history of London Transport: passenger travel and the development of the metropolis. Vol. 1: the nineteenth century*, p.98.

[6] The Reinohl collection is predominantly made up of tickets, but it also includes photographs, journal articles, newspaper cuttings and other ephemera.

There are no notes for chapter 2.

Chapter 3: Shields B type

[1] *Commercial Motor*, 11 November 1911, p. 6.

[2] Select Committee of the House of Commons on Motor Traffic. Proof of Evidence of Mr A. H. Stanley (later Lord Ashfield), April 1913, p. 12. Information from the personal, annotated copy

belonging to Walter J. Iden, Chief Engineer of the London General Omnibus Company. Held in the London Transport Museum Library.

[3] *Commercial Motor*, 10 October 1912, p. 3.

[4] *The Crier of a 100 Towns*, LGOC Marketing Leaflet, c1912, p. 3. The leaflet promotes the sale of advertising space on buses and emphasises the merits of adverts seen on buses travelling across such a wide area.

There are no notes for chapters 4 and 5.

Chapter 6: The 'pirate' buses 1922–33

[1] The bus body was made by Christopher Dodson of Willesden, who also offered independent operators finance arrangements to facilitate purchase of his products.

[2] The main chassis manufacturers were Dennis, Leyland and Straker-Squire. The only chassis not developed from War Office specifications was the Straker-Squire model 'A'.

[3] With the exception of the NS type vehicle, with its cranked chassis frame and low floor level.

[4] Pickup and London Public operated buses from manufacturer Guy.

[5] This was the Associated Daimler Company model 802, developed as the LGOC LS type.

[6] Operator City converted elderly Leyland LBs to six-wheeler buses.

[7] The London Traffic Act, 1924, made pirate practices more difficult by introducing route scheduling and restricting the number of buses on existing routes.

[8] London Public Omnibus Company vehicles were painted in a blue livery.

Chapter 7: Country Bus and Green Line

[1] London Transport was given a virtual monopoly of operating road services within the Special Area and no other operator was allowed to convey passengers locally within the area without London Transport's consent.

[2] The operating department favoured the fitting of a sliding door but were overruled.

There are no notes for chapters 8, 9, 10 and 11.

Chapter 12: Rise of the private car and decline of the bus, 1960–79

[1] Sir Patrick Abercrombie created the County of London Plan (1943) and the Greater London Plan (1944), which both looked forward to the re-conception, and reconstruction, of London after the Second World War. These plans included the proposal for 'New Towns' as satellite developments to London.

[2] The *Greater London Development Plan* was published by the Greater London Council in 1969. It included extensive proposals for new road provision and high-rise developments, which would have seen much of inner suburban London redeveloped on a massive scale.

[3] The 'three-day week' was a strategy by the British government applied during January–March 1974, to conserve electricity at a time of industrial action by mineworkers, who supplied the fuel for current generation in coal-fired power stations.

[4] The 'Winter of Discontent' was the winter of 1978-79, one of the most severe cold periods in Britain since 1962-63. It was characterised politically by widespread strikes of public sector trade unions who demanded larger pay rises, following a number of pay caps.

[5] *The New Works Plan 1935–40*, the second of the Underground Group/London Transport's five year plans, would include substantial extensions to the railway network, and much improved services on the bus system.

[6] The Conservatives retained control of the Greater London Council in 1970, but in 1973 Labour won on a strongly socialist platform. The Conservatives regained control in May 1977, with high profile right wing leader Horace Cutler famous for selling council houses but de-prioritising London Transport.

There are no notes for chapters 13 or 14

TIMELINE

1829 First horse-drawn bus service operated by George Shillibeer starts running on 4 July between Paddington and the Bank. The 'Omnibus' seats around 20 people and is drawn by three horses.

1832 Stage Carriage Act 1832 introduces licencing for buses and allows passengers to be picked up and set down in the City of London for the first time.

1835 Highway Act 1835 requires road traffic to keep to the left hand side of the road.

1838 Drivers and conductors have to be licenced from 10 August 1838 and wear their badges in a prominent position.

1846 Thomas Tilling's bus company starts up in Walworth.

1847 A horse bus with 'knifeboard' seats on the roof appears in the *Illustrated London News* 1 May 1847.

1856 London General Omnibus Company (LGOC) starts operating.

1867 Metropolitan Streets Act 1867 requires passengers to be picked up or set down on the left hand side of the road only. Subsequent bus designs have only one boarding platform, on the near side.

1881 London Road Car Company starts operating; it becomes the second largest horse bus company in London, introducing forward-facing 'garden seat' buses and the first tickets.

1889 Battery electric omnibus is licensed, but not used in public service due to difficulties in recharging.

1891 LGOC bus staff strike over the introduction of tickets, although already in use by London Road Car Company.

1893 Bell Punch ticket machines, used experimentally in 1891, are introduced by the LGOC. Sets of coloured tickets for each fare are printed for every route. Tickets are punched by the conductor and the paper 'confetti' retained in the machine as confirmation of the fare taken.

1899 First motor bus service in London runs from Kennington to Victoria from 9 October 1899, operated by the Motor Traction Company Limited. It is short-lived and withdrawn in 1900.

1902 Motor Traction Company introduces the first London motor bus with solid rubber tyres, a Daimler double-decker.

1904 LGOC operates its first mechanical bus service, using a steam bus.

1905 London Motor Omnibus Company Ltd, the first purely motor bus operator, starts operations 27 March 1905, using the fleet name Vanguard.

1905 LGOC begins using the winged wheel symbol, the forerunner of the roundel, with the name 'General' across it.

1906 Vanguard introduces route numbers; initially on new routes 4 and 5 from 23 April, and then existing routes numbered 1, 2 and 3 from 30 April 1906.

1907 London Motor Omnibus Company merges with associated companies and forms the Vanguard Motor Omnibus Company.

1907 LGOC adopts red as its main livery colour from March 1907.

1908 LGOC absorbs its competitors the London Road Car and Vanguard companies.

1910 LGOC introduces the first mass-produced B type bus, designed by Frank Searle, LGOC Chief Engineer, and built at the company's works in Walthamstow.

1910 Joe Clough, born in Jamaica in 1887, becomes London's first black bus driver, working LGOC B type buses on route 11, between Liverpool Street and Wormwood Scrubs.

1911 First bus map is issued by the LGOC in March 1911.

1911 Last LGOC horse bus operates on 25 October 1911.

1912 Underground Electric Railways Company of London (UERL) obtains financial control of the LGOC.

1912 First LGOC country route begins running between Hounslow and Windsor.

1913 First night buses run in London from 15 July 1913.

1914 Last horse bus operated by Thomas Tilling is withdrawn on the evening of 4 August 1914.

1914 LGOC buses are requisitioned for First World War service from 1 August 1914.

1915 First woman bus conductor in London starts work on 1 November 1915 on Tilling's route 37.

1916 LGOC employs women bus conductors from March 1916.

1919 National Steam Car Company withdraws last steam buses in London.

1919 K type bus introduced, seating 46.

1920 S type bus introduced, with 54 seats. First experimental bus stops are installed by the LGOC on routes 9 and 16 in association with the Police. After the experiment many are retained.

1921 LGOC bus overhaul works opens at Chiswick.

1922 Chocolate Express, the first of the post-war independent bus proprietors begins operating.

1923 NS type bus is introduced in May.

1924 London Traffic Act creates powers to restrict the number of buses on certain streets and establishes the London & Home Counties Traffic Advisory Committee. The Act gives licensing powers to the Metropolitan Police to control the growing number of independent operators.

1924 The Police take on responsibility for allocating route numbers from 1 December.

1925 Pneumatic tyres and covered tops are fitted to buses in London for the first time.

1926 National General Strike in support of the miners stops most bus and tram services in London from 4–11 May.

1927 Last B type buses are withdrawn in October 1927.

1927 First 6 wheeled bus – the LS – is introduced. This class is the first to incorporate an enclosed staircase.

1928 Pneumatic tyres are introduced on double deck buses.

1929 LT type bus is introduced, seating 60 passengers.

1929 ST type bus, the first production buses equipped with enclosed staircases and seating around 50 passengers, introduced.

1930 Road Traffic Act 1930 is passed which, amongst other measures, rules that motor coach services cannot run without restricttions. The Act creates Area Traffic Commissioners to control licences.

1930 Trials of oil (later known as diesel) engines on buses are carried out.

1930 Green Line Coaches Ltd, a subsidiary of LGOC, begins operations.

1932 STL type bus is introduced, with a seating capacity of 56.

1933 London Passenger Transport Board (LPTB) is established by an Act of Parliament with powers to operate all road and underground rail services in the LPTB 'Special Area'. Effective from 1 July 1933.

1934 Oil engine is adopted as future standard power unit for London buses

1935 Fixed bus stops, differentiated as compulsory or request, are installed along every route in the LPTB area..

1937 All bus services are stopped by striking bus crews from 1-27 May. Bus services planned for the Coronation on 12 May are cancelled.

1937 Last solid tyre buses on route 108 run for the last time on 14 April 1937.

1939 RT type bus goes into service in August, and 150 are produced in 1940/41, but quantity production is delayed until after the end of the Second World War.

1940 Women bus conductors are employed again on LPTB road services.

1942 Around 150 ST type double deck buses and a much smaller number of single deck T type buses are equipped with producer gas trailers. The equipment was removed in summer 1944.

1947 Transport Act 1947 creates the British Transport Commission (BTC), bringing LPTB and Britain's railways under national control. LPTB is replaced by a London Transport Executive (LTE). Effective 1 January 1948.

1949 Eight foot wide RTW type bus is introduced.

1950 Last petrol engine bus is withdrawn on 20/21 November 1950.

1951 RF type coach for Green Line services is introduced, seating 39.

1952 Petrol bus engines are replaced by diesel.

1953 Conductors start using Gibson ticket machines to issue tickets.

1954 Routemaster bus (RM type), with seats for 64, is displayed on 24 September 1954 for the first time at the Commercial Motor Show at Earl's Court.

1956 Overhaul of bus bodies and chassis is transferred from Chiswick to a new and larger works at Aldenham. Chiswick is subsequently redesigned to deal with reconditioning of engines and mechanical and electrical units.

1956 London Bus Week is held to celebrate the centenary of the LGOC.

1957 Red Rover tickets are introduced in October 1957.

1958 Bus crews strike from 5 May 1958 over pay and conditions. Full services do not resume until 21 June.

1959 Routemaster buses begin to enter regular service, replacing trolleybuses as the latter are progressively withdrawn.

1961 30ft long version of Routemaster (RML type) and seating 72 enters service.

1962 Transport Act 1962 is passed, which abolishes the LTE and creates an autonomous London Transport Board (LTB) from 1 January 1963.

1962 Double deck Routemasters with coach seating (RMC type) are introduced on some Green Line services.

1964 Illuminated advertisements are fitted on some Routemasters.

1965 Trials begin with 30ft long 72 seat Leyland Atlantean (XA) and Daimler Fleetline (XF) buses.

1965 RCL type, 30ft long Routemasters with coach seating, come into service at Grays and Romford garages from 2 June 1965.

1965 RC type coaches, 36ft long, introduced on Green Line services from 28 November 1965.

1966 Red Arrow service between Victoria and Marble Arch starts on 18 April using 36ft long 'standee' single deck buses (XMS type) able to carry 73 passengers (25 seated and 48 standing).

1966 Last RTW type bus runs in May on routes from Brixton garage.

1967 Trials begin in August with front entrance, rear engine Routemaster bus (FRM) from Tottenham garage.

1968 Production of Routemasters ends.

1968 First Country area MB buses enter service on route 447 from Reigate garage on 9 March.

1968 The first phase of the long term plan to reshape London's bus services based on a network of local 'flat-fare' services is introduced in Wood Green and Walthamstow.

1968 Last RTL type bus is withdrawn from service at Willesden Garage on 29 November.

1969 Transport (London) Act 1969 replaces LTB with a London Transport Executive (LTE), responsible to the Greater London Council (GLC), for operating the Central (red) buses and the Underground. Country (green) bus and Green Line coach services are transferred to National Bus Company subsidiary London Country Bus Services Ltd.

1970 Trials of buses equipped with two way radio begin, to combat traffic congestion problems.

1971 One person operated double deck bus 'The Londoner' (DMS type) enters passenger service with accommodation for 89 passengers (68 seated and 21 standing).

1971 Last single deck buses with conductors run on 16 April on route 236.

1971 Smoking on single deck London buses is banned in May, following a campaign by Action on Smoking and Health (ASH). On double deck buses, smoking is still allowed in the rear part of the upper deck.

1974 Jill Viner becomes London Transport's first woman bus driver in June, based at Norbiton garage in south west London and driving an RT type vehicle.

1979 Last RT type buses are withdrawn from Barking Garage in April 1979.

1984 London Regional Transport (LRT) is created to replace the LTE, reporting to the Secretary of State for Transport. London buses are no longer controlled by a London based authority.

1985 LRT sets up a subsidiary, London Buses Limited (LBL), to run its bus services.

1985 First bus routes run by private operators as a result of tendering process.

1986 Greater London Council is finally abolished.

1986 Aldenham Works closes in November 1986.

1988 Chiswick Works is sold, and demolished by 1990.

1991 A total ban on smoking on buses comes into force on 14 February.

1994 Trials of low-floor, accessible buses commence on London United route 120 from 29 January.

2000 Transport for London (TfL) is created, effective from 3 July.

2000 From 1 September all new double and single deck buses are required to have wheelchair access to comply with the Disability Discrimination Act.

2000 Low-floor buses become mandatoryas routes are routinely re-tendered by LBL

2003 Oyster card for payment of fares is launched in July.

2005 52 people are killed in bomb attacks on three Underground trains and a bus on 7 July.

2005 Last Routemaster bus in regular service runs on 9 December.

2005 The articulated or 'bendy' bus enters service. Accessible to wheelchair users and carrying almost double the number of passengers of a Routemaster, they were not universally popular and were eventually withdrawn after 9 December 2011.

2006 From 23 December 2006 all buses on regular services are required to be step free and accessible.

2006 Single deck diesel-electric 'hybrid' buses are introduced in March. Double deck hybrid vehicles are introduced in January 2007.

2007 Decision is taken by TfL to remove the distinction between compulsory and request stops.

2010 The first hydrogen bus is launched on 10 December on route RV1.

2012 The first New Routemaster bus enters service on 27 February 2012.

2012 Contactless card payment for fares begins on buses 13 December 2012.

2013 Route 24 between Hampstead Heath and Pimlico is the first to fully convert to the New Routemaster bus in June.

2013 Trial of battery-electric buses begins in December.

2014 A cavalcade of 48 buses old and new parades down Regent Street on 22 June as part of Year of the Bus celebrations.

2014 Contactless smartcards can be used on buses; from 6 July 2014 cash payments for fares are no longer accepted.

FURTHER READING

Books

Akehurst, Laurie. *Country Buses: Volume one, 1933-1949*. n.p. : Capital Transport Publishing, 2012.

Akehurst, Laurie. *Country Buses: Volume two, 1950-1959*. n.p. : Capital Transport Publishing, 2014.

Akehurst, Laurie. *London Transport Green Line*. Harrow: Capital Transport, 2005.

Aldridge, John. *London Transport Bus Garages*. Hersham: Ian Allan, 2001.

Arnold, Barry and Harris, Mike. *Reshaping London's Buses*. Harrow Weald: Capital Transport, 1982.

Barker, T.C. and Robbins, Michael. *A History of London Transport: Passenger Travel and the Development of the Metropolis. Vol. 1, The Nineteenth Century. London : Allen & Unwin, 1963; Vol. 2, The Twentieth Century to 1970*. London: Allen & Unwin, 1974.

Barman, Christian. *The Man Who Built London Transport: a Biography of Frank Pick*. Newton Abbot: David & Charles, 1979.

Beard, Tony. *The Birth of the RT*. n.p. : Capital Transport Publishing, 2011.

Blacker, Ken. *RT: Story of a London Bus*. Harrow Weald: Capital Transport Publishing, 1979.

Blacker, Ken. *The STLs*. Harrow Weald: Capital Transport Publishing, 1984.

Blacker, Ken. *Routemaster. Volume One, 1954-1969*. Harrow Weald: Capital Transport Publishing, 1991.

Blacker, Ken. *Routemaster. Volume Two, 1970-2005*. Harrow Weald: Capital Transport Publishing, 2007.

Blacker, Ken. *The London ST*. n.p. : Capital Transport Publishing, 2012.

Blacker, Ken, Lunn, Ron and Westgate, Reg. *London's Buses. Volume One, The Independent Era – 1922-1934*. St. Albans: H J Publications, 1977.

Blacker, Ken, Lunn, Ron and Westgate, Reg. *London's Buses. Volume Two, Country Independents – 1919-1939*. St. Albans: H J Publications, 1983.

Bruce, J Graeme and Curtis, Colin H. *The London Motor Bus: Its Origins and Development*. London: London Transport Executive, 1973.

Curtis, Colin H. *Buses of London*. London: London Transport, 1979.

Curtis, Colin H. *The Routemaster Bus: a Comprehensive History of a Highly Successful London Bus Type From its Design, Development and Introduction Into the Fleet*. Speldhurst: Midas Books, 1981.

Curtis, Colin H. *40 Years with London Transport*. Glossop: Transport Publishing Company, 1990.

Day, John R. *The Story of the London Bus: London and its Buses from the Horse Bus to the Present Day*. London: London Transport Executive, 1973.

Elborough, Travis. *The Bus We Loved: London's Affair With the Routemaster*. London:

Granta, 2005.

Glancey, Jonathan. *Douglas Scott*. London: The Design Council, 1988.

Glazier, Ken. *London Buses and the Second World War*. 2nd ed. Harrow Weald: Capital Transport Publishing, 1991.

Glazier, Ken. *RF*. Harrow Weald: Capital Transport Publishing, 1991.

Glazier, Ken. *London Buses Before the War*. Harrow Weald: Capital Transport Publishing, 1995.

Glazier, Ken. *The Last Years of the General*: [London buses 1930-1933]. Harrow Weald: Capital Transport Publishing, 1995.

Glazier, Ken. *London Bus File 1955-1962*. Harrow Weald: Capital Transport Publishing, 1998.

Glazier, Ken. *Routes to Recovery: [London buses 1945-1952]*. Harrow Weald: Capital Transport Publishing, 2000.

Glazier, Ken. *The Battles of the General*. Harrow Weald: Capital Transport Publishing, 2003.

Glazier, Ken. *London Transport Garages*. Harrow: Capital Transport Publishing, 2006.

Gray, John A. *London's 1960s Buses: a Class Album*. Harrow Weald: Capital Transport Publishing, 2008.

Green, Oliver, and Reed, John. *The London Transport Jubilee Book 1933-1983*. London: Daily Telegraph, 1983.

Hibbs, John. *The History of British Bus Services.* 2nd ed. Newton Abbot: David & Charles, 1989.

Jones, D W K, and Davis B J. *Green Line 1930-1980.* Reigate: London Country Bus Services, 1980.

Kidner, R W. *The London Motor Bus 1896-1975.* 5th rev. ed. Blandford: Oakwood Press, 1975.

Latchford, A L, and Pollins, H. *London General: the Story of the London Bus 1856-1956.* London: London Transport, 1956.

Lawrence, David. *London Transport Cap Badges.* Harrow Weald: Capital Transport, 1989.

Lawrence, David. *A Logo for London.* London: Laurence King, 2013.

Lee, Charles E. *The Horse Bus as a Vehicle.* London: British Transport Commission, 1962.

Lee, Charles E. *The Early Motor Bus.* London: London Transport Executive, 1974.

Lewin, Tony. *London's New Routemaster.* London: Merrell, 2014.

London Transport Board. *A Report on London's Bus Services and London Transport's Plans for Reshaping Them.* London: London Transport Board, 1966.

Moore, H C. *Omnibuses and Cabs: Their Origin and History.* London: Chapman & Hall, 1902.

Newman, Stanley. *"Overground": a Pictorial Half-century of London's Road Transport.* London: Ian Allan, 1947.

Reed, John. *London Buses Past and Present.* Middlesex: Capital Transport Publishing, 1988.

Reed, John. *London Buses : a Brief History.* Harrow: Capital Transport Publishing, 2007.

Robbins, George. *Tilling in London.* Harrow Weald: Capital Transport, 1986.

Robbins, George. *General Buses of the Twenties: an Introduction to the K, S, NS, LS Classes.* Malvern: Images Publishing in association with John A S Hambley, 1996.

Robbins, George and Atkinson, J.B. *The London B-type Motor Omnibus.* 3rd rev. ed. Twickenham: World of Transport, 1991.

Rotondaro, Anna. *Women at Work on London's Transport 1905-1978.* Stroud: Tempus Publishing, 2004.

Sekon, G A. *Locomotion in Victorian London.* London: Oxford University Press, 1938.

Taylor, Hugh. *London Trolleybus Routes.* Harrow Weald: Capital Transport, 1994.

Vanguard: a Symposium: An Important Chapter in the Early History of the London Motorbus. London: London Historical Research Group, The Omnibus Society, 2001.

Wagstaff, J S. *The London Country Bus.* Blandford: The Oakwood Press, 1968.

Wallis, Philip. *London's Night Buses: Volume One, 1913-1983.* London: Modern Transport, 2011.

Wallis, Philip. *London's Night Buses: Volume Two, 1984-2013.* London: Modern Transport, 2013.

Ward, William D. Ole Bill: *London Buses and the First World War.* London: London Transport Museum, 2014.

Warren, Kenneth. *The Motorbus in London Country.* Shepperton: Ian Allan, 1984.

Journals
Automotor Journal
Classic Bus
Commercial Motor
Industrial Motor Review
London Bus Magazine
Motor Car Journal
Motor Traction
Tramway and Railway World

Staff magazines
TOT
Pennyfare
London Transport Magazine
LT News

Websites
www.busmap.co.uk/
www.eplates.info/maps/general.html
www.londonbusmuseum.com/
www.psvbadges.co.uk/
middx.net/aec/index.htm
www.ltmuseum.co.uk/

AUTHOR BIOGRAPHIES

Laurie Akehurst

Laurie Akehurst joined London Transport as a junior clerk and having worked in a variety of disciplines within the organisation became a manager with London Underground prior to opting for early retirement. Laurie was elected a member of the Chartered Institute of Transport in 1972 and is interested in researching transport history and operations. A London Transport Museum Friends' volunteer since 2001 Laurie is a curatorial volunteer and serves as a Friends' representative on several committees. Since 2001 Laurie has written various books on the history of London Transport's former Country Buses and Green Line coaches.

Leon Daniels

After a spell in the Civil Service, Leon entered London's transport story unconventionally, by joining the late Prince Marshall's Obsolete Fleet which ran a fleet of red buses on specialist tourist services on behalf of London Transport. In due course he ran his own sightseeing tour bus business which was eventually absorbed into Ensignbus. There then followed entry into the tendered bus market which grew rapidly. The business changed hands as it expanded, owned latterly in Hong Kong. He led a management buy-out which then in turn was sold to FirstGroup plc. He spent 13 years at First as a member of the UK Bus Board with various responsibilities in UK and overseas including as Commercial Director. In 2011 he was appointed MD Surface Transport at TfL and is responsible not only for London's bus service but also cycling, taxis, boats and the operation of the road network. In some way this consummated a lifelong interest in transport in London which has also resulted in his own contribution to the historic vehicle movement having been a part owner of an old London bus for some 40 years.

Roger French

Roger French has had a lifelong interest in buses. Born and growing up in London in the 1950s and 1960s he followed developments affecting London Transport with particular attention. As a student he worked at 55 Broadway and as a conductor at Palmers Green garage between 1970 and 1974 followed by a career in provincial bus companies before becoming Managing Director of the Brighton & Hove Bus Company where he worked for 31 years until his retirement in 2013. He was awarded an OBE for services to public transport in 2005 and wrote a book Pride & Joy in 2010.

Oliver Green

Oliver Green is former Head Curator of London Transport Museum and became the museum's first Research Fellow in 2009. He was brought up in North Finchley, an area of suburban London where trolleybuses always seemed to outnumber buses in the 1950s before the arrival of the Routemaster. He has lectured and published widely on various aspects of London's transport history, his most recent book being *Frank Pick's London: art, design and the modern city* published by the Victoria & Albert Museum in association with London Transport Museum in 2013.

David Lawrence

Dr David Lawrence is an historian and writer interested in all places where people, movement and design meet. He is Research Fellow at the London Transport Museum, the author and editor of several books including *A Logo for London* (2013), *Bright Underground Spaces* (2008) and *Underground Architecture* (1994), and is Associate Professor at a London university. David is a Fellow of the Royal Geographical Society.

Sam Mullins

Sam Mullins has been Director of the London Transport Museum since 1994, overseeing its development as amuseum telling the social history of transport in London, past, present and future. Milestones have included creating the first publicly accessible museum store in the UK at Acton Depot in 1999, the redevelopment of the Covent Garden site in 2007, transition to charity governance in 2008, creation of the Tube150 programme for 2013, which returned steam services to the tunnels opened in 1863, and the Year of the Bus in 2014, celebrating the contribution of the red bus to London.

Simon Murphy

Simon Murphy grew up on the 32 route, went to school on the 143, and has lived at the intersection of the 25 and the 308 for the last twenty years. He discovered London on Red Bus Rover tickets in the late 1970s, usually starting with a 113 to Oxford Circus. Inspired by 1970s punk and DIY culture, he has self-published a diverse range of magazines and comics since the 1980s, also playing in bands, and collecting records and 1950s electric guitars. He has worked as a curator at London Transport Museum since 1989. His favourite bus in the collection is the GS type.

Richard Peskett

Born in Haslemere, Surrey in 1946, Richard took an interest in transport from an early age. His grandmother, who lived with his family at the time, used to tell him stories about London in her childhood during the late 1800s, the days of horse buses, hansoms and growlers. A local coal merchant had kept all his early motor lorries in a shed and these could be seen from the road, all creating a fascination in the subject for Richard. Brought up in a family world of building but interests at heart were in transport and engineering. Bought and sold government surplus for several years then turned a hobby into a full time business of vehicle restoration, which has continued ever since. Customers have included London Transport Museum, Louwman Collection, Mercedes-Benz. Historical research from contemporary material and collecting original photographic images is a priority interest nowadays.

Tim Shields

Tim Shields has worked as a Curator at the London Transport Museum since 2004. Specialising in early bus and rail vehicles he was responsible for project managing the restoration of B type motor bus B2737. He regularly gives museum talks on vehicle preservation and operation.

Mike A Sutcliffe, MBE, FCA

Mike is a Chartered Accountant with a lifelong interest in historic road vehicles and is well known for his preservation and restoration of ten of the oldest buses in the world, all totally derelict when found and authentically restored to almost new condition. It was for 'Services to Motor Heritage' that he was awarded the MBE. He is Secretary and Editor of The Leyland Society, having produced 80 magazines and books, he is a Council Member of The Transport Trust and a Trustee of the National Association of Road Transport Museums. Over the last 55 years he has collected a large quantity of original material and photographs relating to the history of the motor bus, covering all operations in the UK.

Roger Torode

Roger Torode had a 30-year career with London Transport in the bus and central departments. Starting in Business Planning, he then led the testing of drivers' electronic ticket machines and the experimental Autocheck system. He became Manager at Walthamstow garage and Commercial Director of London Forest Travel. Roger was asked to evaluate contactless smartcard technology which led to the Harrow trial in 1994 and, with parallel work on London Underground, to the Oyster card. In 1997 he was appointed European Affairs Manager, working with the International Public Transport Association (UITP). After 2004, he assisted the Public Carriage Office in reviewing the Conditions of Fitness for London taxis, before retiring from LT to work as a consultant. He jointly authored the book *Midland Red Style* and is now writing a study of the privatisation of London's buses.

Caroline Warhurst

Caroline joined the Museum as Librarian in 2002, following more than 20 years in local authority reference and local history libraries. The Museum library supports all aspects of the Museum's work and the breadth and depth of the collection makes it a hugely rewarding one to work with. It is the emerging transport story of London's Victorian era however that has always held particular interest for Caroline. In pursuing this interest, she has been fortunate to benefit from the knowledge provided by the late and highly respected bus experts, David Ruddom and Ken Glazier, both of whom worked in the library on the bus routes database and other projects. The Routes project continues today in the library, ably supported by Laurie Akehurst and Brian Polley.

ACKNOWLEDGEMENTS

To cover the extensive social history of the London bus in detail, drawing on the resources of the London Transport Museum and Transport for London, has been an exciting and challenging project with a very pleasing result. A work of this magnitude requires the input of a host of contributors and other professionals.

Transport for London (TfL) and London Transport Museum would like to thank our invited authors for the time and thought they have given to this project; also for the inclusion of items from their personal collections to enhance the publication. They are Laurie Akehurst, Roger French, Oliver Green, David Lawrence, Richard Peskett, Mike Sutcliffe and Roger Torode.

We are grateful to Leon Daniels at TfL for supporting and contributing to this work. The staff at London Transport Museum have also contributed chapters and thanks are due in particular to: Sam Mullins, Director, for initiating and steering the collaboration; Dr David Lawrence, LTM Research Fellow for editing the book; Simon Murphy, Curator, for picture research; Tim Shields, Curator, for the B type chapter, and Caroline Warhurst, Librarian, for managing the copy-editing process. Finally, our thanks go to Sau-Fun Mo, Head of Design, for the vibrant design which supports this unique story.

INDEX